Multi-coloured Maze

Marjorie Dobson

**Drama, hymns, prayers and poems
for worship and everyday living**

Stainer & Bell

First published in 2004 by Stainer & Bell Limited
23 Gruneisen Road, London N3 1DZ

British Library Cataloguing-in-Publication Data
A catalogue record for this book is available from the British Library

ISBN 0 85249 882 9

Cover photograph © Copyright Colin Anderson, brandxpictures
www.brandxpictures.com

Printed in Great Britain by Caligraving Ltd, Thetford

Contents

Preface

Anyone who reads this book but skips the author's Introduction will have to go to the last page to discover the context for its title, but that is the pattern of the collection and, I believe, of its author too – experience comes first and reflection upon it and extension of it follows.

I have known Marjorie Dobson for many years and am delighted to be associated with this book. The hymns, poems and dramatic scripts offered here have been forged out of her experience as a jobbing preacher of the gospel. In her attempts to translate gospel values into worship experiences, to lift small groups of jaded pilgrims to new endeavours in faith and to encourage new insights into the work of grace in the lives of ordinary people, Marjorie has uncovered a rich resource for many of her fellow preachers. That she allows us to see the 'working out' of how many of these pieces came to be written is an additional joy.

The author leads us through one of the ways in which people experience God and the Church. Entering through the Church's celebration of the Christian Year of festivals, Christmas, Easter and Pentecost, we then discover the joys of the Bible, explore the way of discipleship that renews and transforms family life and discover the nature of and responsibility within the global family of which we are a part.

Marjorie Dobson offers us words that articulate and encapsulate the glimpses of eternal truths we stumble upon when we seek to walk the Christian way and does so in a manner that enables shared participation in the expression of them. These are mostly designed to be used with congregations, but will also stimulate personal devotion.

In the last hymn of this book, the hope is expressed that the interweaving of all our lives will be part of God's eternal purposes. The contribution of this book will be to add a significant thread.

Kathleen Richardson
The Reverend Baroness Richardson of Calow

Author's Introduction

'Multi-coloured maze' is how you could describe my life, experiences, faith and certainly my writing, which is why this anthology is a personal one, with a whole range of material of all sizes, shapes, tones and colours. It is the only way that a collection of my work could be produced. There are not quite enough hymns for a hymn collection. There are several 'performance pieces' of different kinds, but not enough for a book full of drama. There is poetry and perhaps enough of it for a small anthology, but it would not be a true reflection of the other work. There are prayers and blessings, but they would need to be counted in the hundreds to fill a book and I have not written so many – yet. There are even examples of complete services of worship, although I have not gone to the extreme of including the sermons for these – for which act you may be thankful.

It would have been difficult for any publisher to categorise this collection clearly, which is why it was suggested that it should have a personal life of its own. Some of this work has been published in anthologies of worship material, obviously following the theme set by the editor of each book. Hymns have been written for occasions, or people, or because I could not find a suitable hymn on the subject. Drama has been demanded for illustration, or to add to a special service. Poetry is more inspirational and comes out of the blue sometimes, but some of it has been written for competitions, or by request. The sideways way of looking at some things, which occasionally produces a wry smile, is part of my personality and will insist in coming out in the writing, though not necessarily in the more serious pieces.

So this complex character with a mind that buzzes around in all kind of different directions at once is bound to produce a real multi-coloured maze, if ever there was one. I hope that, as you thread your way through the variety of this work, you will find something of use, or interest, or help, or inspiration.

As in any baffling maze, the paths in this book mix, cross, run alongside each other and intermingle at times. But, unlike other mazes, all these paths eventually lead to the same central place where we meet with God. The variety of paths reflects that variety we find in life and recognises that we make different approaches to God depending on our personal experiences. Yet –

> Though we never see the picture
> with your sense of space and time,
> help us, Lord, to take our places
> in our faith's continuing line,
> as all lives are interwoven
> in your final grand design.

Marjorie Dobson

This book is dedicated to my husband Ron,
who had confidence in my writing ability
long before I had the skill to justify it.

The Festival Way

The major Christian festivals are a way in to the church for many people. Parents and grandparents love to visit the nativity play, or carol service, to see their children performing. Easter is not quite so popular, except where there are Holy Week pageants or drama, or when the church is specially decorated on Easter Day. Pentecost is a bit of a mystery, even to some faithful church attenders, although it used to be celebrated with processions of children dressed in white and the day was known affectionately as Whit Sunday. Many older people remember those days, but probably would not be able to link the celebrations with the events of that first Christian Pentecost.

How do we cope with this irregular influx of people? Some say we should be sure to always give them the familiar hymns and worship material, so that they know that the church is an unchanging presence in a constantly changing world. If that were true, none of this material would ever have been written. The alternative is to try to create new ways of looking at our story and message, ways that have relevance to the culture and language of our everyday society.

The following pieces in this 'Festival Way' section are offered in an attempt to shed fresh light on familiar stories, or to put flesh on the bones of the people involved. Finding a new viewpoint from which to consider an annual event is a constant problem. Perhaps some of these writings will help to do that.

Advent and Christmas

BIRTH BRINGS A PROMISE

NEWBORN (11.10.11.10.)   *Basil E. Bridge (1927–)*

Birth brings a pro-mise of new life a-wak-ing, dawn-ing of
hope through a child's o-pen eyes. Un-chart-ed fu-ture is
there for the mak-ing, chal-lenge and change in a ba-by's first cries.

BIRTH brings a promise of new life awaking,
dawning of hope through a child's open eyes.
Uncharted future is there for the making,
challenge and change in a baby's first cries.

Every new life changes those who are round it
making demands of commitment and care,
calling for love to enfold and surround it,
reshaping patterns by claiming a share.

Jesus the newborn crossed time's moving stages
changing their course by the act of his birth,
translating God from the mystery of ages,
rooting our faith by his presence on earth.

Wonder and worship were waiting to greet him,
love and devotion were his to command,
life was transformed for the ones sent to meet him,
touching their God in a child's outstretched hand.

Birth gives a promise of new life awaking.
Jesus the newborn calls us to new birth.
All that he promised is ours for the taking
when our commitment brings God down to earth.

Although writers are rarely completely satisfied with their work and often wish they had changed key words or phrases before they went into print, this hymn is one of the rare exceptions to this rule. Apart from one alteration suggested by the editor of 'Worship Live', in which it first appeared, the rest of the piece has remained as it was first written.

The challenge to write it had been made by a student chaplain friend, who needed a carol to use with his university student group. 'It should not mention, stars, angels, shepherds, kings or even stables.' In other words, cut out the trimmings and get down to the basic fact of the incarnation. Two lines from Charles Wesley's 'Let earth and heaven combine' have always summed up the whole story for me –

> *'Our God contracted to a span,*
> *Incomprehensibly made man.'*

They may not be the easiest of phrases to sing, but they put the vital truth into nine words. However much the story has been dressed up, the fact remains that the Son of God was born into a humble family with parents who took on the task of nurturing him until he took on his ministry. What a difference that must have made to their lives. First-time parents find themselves disturbed by a whole range of new emotions and challenges and that would have been no different for Mary and Joseph. This excitement and wonder is reflected in the words.

But the birth of Jesus changed more than the life of that particular family. God broke into history in a new way and changed its course forever. Jesus challenges us to bring God down to earth, for those around us, by our commitment to his way of living.

Although this was definitely written as a Christmas hymn it has frequently been used at services of infant baptism since it was published in 'NewStart Hymns and Songs' in 1999. That is understandable, given the nature of the words in the first two verses, but I often wonder whether the other verses make any impact on baptismal visitors who may not be regular church attenders.

The 11.10.11.10. metre was chosen because I have always enjoyed the different tunes set to the carol 'Brightest and best of the sons of the morning', although those words are often sung without much understanding of some of the more archaic phraseology. A new tune – NEWBORN – was written by Basil E. Bridge, after the piece had first appeared in 'Worship Live'.

ADVENT

This meditation was written around the same time as the hymn 'Birth brings a promise' and it is easy to see that the same thought processes were at work on this piece. The West Yorkshire Synod of the Methodist Church has produced a series of booklets of prayers for various occasions and circumstances and they were always written by people from the District. As we were living there at the time, I was asked to contribute to two of these books, the first being 'Open with God', in which this meditation first appeared.

WAITING for the birth of a first child is always a special time.
There are many questions, but they all merge into one.
'What difference will this child make to our world?'

We are once again waiting to celebrate your birth, Lord, and the question is
    still the same,
'What difference will this child make to our world?'

Jesus, we thank you for the way you came into the world as a baby and grew to be an adult. We are grateful that you understood it was difficult for us to picture God until put into human terms. We recognise with gladness the familiar stories of Christmas, the sense of excitement and anticipation in the air and the celebrations of the season. Your coming into the world was a very special occasion and we can all exclaim with delight at the birth of this baby.

But babies change the lives of those around them – and babies grow up.

In our celebrations, Lord, help us to remember that you changed the world and
    that you will change us too, if we grow along with you.

Your picture of God helps us to understand him.
Your call challenges us to live for him.
Your behaviour and teaching give us a pattern for living.
Your love reaches out and envelops us.
Your death brought forgiveness.
Your resurrection fires hope.
Your Spirit sustains our daily living.
We can never be the same again,
once we have accepted you into our lives.

Christ of the Advent hope,
be with us as we celebrate the difference your birth has made in the world and give us the vision and courage we need to spread this exciting good news to others.

THREE WOMEN

Although the men get most of the public recognition in the story of Jesus there is much evidence of the contribution made by women, especially in Luke's Gospel. The detailed story of Mary and the account of her meeting with Elizabeth are only given by Luke, but are told with great understanding of the emotions experienced by the women. These emotions are explored further in these pieces spoken by the two women.

But there were other women around at the time too. The innkeeper's wife is a purely imaginary figure, but a most likely person to have been there, especially if she knew she had a heavily pregnant woman as one of her guests – however humble was the accommodation they were offered. These unknown figures surrounding the events of the life of Jesus are a gift to writers, who can manipulate them to suit whatever message they think is appropriate at the time. You will find many of them in the following pages.

This piece was written for spoken performance and has been used in many services and events in the Christmas season. Mary and Elizabeth should be read by women of suitable ages. The innkeeper's wife could be any age, but is at least in her middle years. The words 'soon I will be gone' are meant to signify her moving on, although they could be that of a much older woman preparing for death. It might be wise not to mention this to the reader.

Elizabeth

I STILL find it hard to believe!
Me! At my age!

And I know what they're saying about me in the village
and what they used to say.
The whispering behind my back when we all gathered at the well.
At first I didn't mind –
it was all good-humoured –
though that was in the days when I was young
and thought my time would come one day!
But as the years went by it hurt me more,
especially the pity in the eyes of those
whose children followed them each day.
The knowing looks and disapproving stares
of those old women watching as I passed –
their grandchildren safe, playing around their skirts.
Oh, how I longed for children of my own.
The bitter tears I wept night after night
after each day of thoughtless, questioning eyes.
My prayers were all the same, but fruitless too.
Almost as if God could not hear my pain.
I'd given in!

But on that day my husband came back home
so strange and dazed and speechless and amazed,
I took him in my arms and loved him then
with tenderness and warmth to give him strength
and though he could not speak a word, I knew
that God had spoken.

My time is drawing near.
Only a month or two and then … a son!
I know! A very special baby boy!
One I must cherish through his early years
for God has laid his hand on him already.
I will not have him always.
But that is God's way
and he must prepare it first through me.
I still find it hard to believe.

Mary

I STILL find it hard to believe!
Me! At my age!

And I know what they're saying about me in the village
and what they used to say.
The whispering behind my back when we all gathered at the well.
As if they thought I couldn't hear –
except for those who wanted me to know
how much they disapproved
and those who spat out their opinions
of one who could behave as I did, when so young.
Of course, they didn't understand what happened.
Neither did I, in that first puzzling hour.
The voice of God speaking to one like me,
so young and all the prospect of my life before me.
Promised in marriage.
Love's fulfilment still to come.
All the bright days – and suddenly, this shadow!
The unexpected, unbelievable, yet true!
What could I say?

All my young life I had wanted God to use me,
prayed with devotion, served him with true heart.
But this way? Oh, my God!
Yet how could I refuse him?
If God needs me – then who am I to choose?

My time is drawing near and then … a son!
I know! A very special baby boy!
One I must cherish through his early years
for God he is and was and is to be.
And all the joy of loving his first early years is mine
and all the promise of his future life –
the days when he will go to change the world.
I hope that all the prophecies do not come true
for his sake – and for mine.
Yet one of them is happening now, through me!
I still find it hard to believe.

The Innkeeper's Wife

I STILL find it hard to believe!
Me! At my age!

And I know what they're saying about me in the village
and what they used to say.
But I can't help that!
In my trade your life is never normal
and no matter how hard you try to keep the family together
you haven't always the time to take as much care as the others.
And when you've been in this business all your life,
you think you've seen everything because you keep an inn.
The drunks, the desperate, the accommodating women,
the passing trade of every shape and size,
the travellers on their Temple pilgrimage,
the tradesmen who will sell you anything.
I've got a hundred tales to tell – and more.
Yet still they caught me out.
I felt sorry for them when they turned up at my door.
We were packed out, no inch of space to breathe –
and you could see at once the girl was desperate.
So near her time, I thought she would have it on my doorstep.
What could I do, but show them to the stable?
At least it was warm and dry and she could have her child in peace –
and that's what inns are for – for shelter and protection.
But when at last I managed to draw breath
and had the time to see that all was well,
as soon as I got near the door I knew –
a son – a very special baby boy.
I knew that God had laid his hand on him –
those shepherds and that star convinced me too!
God had used me! What else could I have done?

My time is drawing near.
Soon I will be gone.
The rest of them are glad to see me go.
How could I know how Herod would react?
I'm not a politician – only the wife of an innkeeper.
But I still know that what I did was right.
That child will grow in safety, thanks to me.
And God must use him in a special way –
why else did all this happen? But ...
I still find it hard to believe.

WERE WE THERE?

Isn't it irritating to read a poem, which has instant appeal, but also makes a point, and then not be able to find it again when you need it? That is how this poem came to be written.

It was some years ago that I read a piece written from the point of view of a guest at the inn where Jesus was born, who left the next morning without recognising that anything unusual had happened. Later, when there was a slot in a Christmas service that was just made for the piece, I could not remember who wrote it, or in which book I'd seen it. The only way to resolve the problem was to write another version of it. Although this contains the same germ of the idea, there is no intention of copying the original, and the language and speech patterns expressed here must be different, as we each have our own way of expressing the same thoughts.

IF ONLY we'd known
as we crowded into the inn that night,
pushing and shoving to get our places!
We were determined not to be left out in the cold,
so we arrived early.

The innkeeper and his wife were harassed
as they packed us in,
squeezing our blankets into the smallest space,
rushing our food
and pushing us from the tables
to feed the following crowd.

How good it was to rest
after that wearying journey.
The Romans didn't care
how much it cost us to get there,
either in terms of money, or of time.
What did it matter to them
that we'd had to travel the length of the country?
Did they assume
we'd all stayed in the birthplace of our fathers?

So when we arrived
we were glad to find a place
and so concerned with our own welfare,
we had no time for others.
The inn was warm,
the food was good,
we met old friends,
the wine flowed freely
and we were only thankful
it was not us that the innkeeper had to put into the stable
because the inn was full.

We did not sleep well that night.
There were too many people
in too little space
and the smells and sounds were incredible!
But we heard nothing outside.
We saw no lights in the sky,
heard no sounds from the stable,
except the animals
and a far-off baby's cry,
which was nothing to what we heard inside the inn!

So, next morning we left,
packing our bags and paying the bill
and glad to get out into the air again
to finish our journey,
register our names
and turn around to face the road to home.
If only we'd known!

But how could we?
Bethlehem seemed the same that night
as any other.
And we were not aware
there had even been a birth!

THE STARS SHONE DOWN

THURSTASTON (D.C.M.)

Christopher Maxim (1971–)

The stars shone down to wel-come Christ on his first night on earth and one star, bright - est of them all, blazed for Mes-si - ah's birth. No roy-al cra - dle wel-comed him, no robes of state were worn. But in the out-house of an inn the Prince of Peace was born.

Descant

Around the fields of Bethlehem
great angel voices rang
and startled shepherds left their sheep
to hear the words they sang.
'Good news, great joy and peace is come.
A child is born this night
whose life and death will change the world
and you will see this sight.'

From Eastern lands the wise men came
to greet this newborn king,
though shadows hung around the gifts
they brought to honour him.
Their dreams and visions drew them on
past Herod's jealous eye.
Their pilgrimage of faith and hope
led by that star-strewn sky.

So may we in this present time
be constantly aware
that God still comes in human form
to those who trust and care.
May we, like shepherds, hear his voice:
like wise men, travel far
to find our faith newborn again
beneath that Christmas star.

This hymn was an entry to a competition in the 'Writers' News' magazine. The brief was for a carol to the tune FOREST GREEN containing no more than three verses and the competition judge was a Methodist Minister named Andrew Pratt. Although I knew his name and some of his work, I had not met Andrew when this piece was written and judged, but he must have seen some merit in it, as it was shortlisted for consideration, though not an actual prizewinner.

You may have noticed that the hymn does not stick to the competition brief because it has four verses. This is one of those cases of not reading the rules closely enough until ten days before the final competition entry date. At that point I had to perform a quick rearrangement of the lines to reduce four verses to three. Once the competition was over and there was no danger of the magazine printing the three-verse version, it was restored to its original shape. When I became a fellow member of the northern editorial team for 'Worship Live', I confessed this mistake to Andrew, who had by that time completely forgotten the whole competition. However he did agree to read through a batch of my material and to offer advice on it. That advice and encouragement has been a great help in this work.

This carol stands firmly in the mainstream, with stars, angels, shepherds and wise men all firmly in place. The last verse is also traditional in feel, as many carols end with the call to remember how the events of Christmas affect our lives today.

SING A SONG OF JESUS

When the material was being gathered for the children's song book 'Sound Bytes' (Stainer & Bell, 1999), the editor Andrew Pratt contacted contributors to the 'Worship Live' periodical to ask for material suitable for children from the age of eight upwards. This was not an easy request to fulfil, as only one of my hymns had been written for an all-age group and none had been written specifically for children. But the challenge was there and needed a response.

Around this time I had taken a Christmas service with children and used the story of Michael Mouse from the 'Wild Goose Prints' collection of the Iona Community. This involved having the children performing the sound effects of all the different animals and they had thoroughly enjoyed themselves. By some strange process this led to the idea of using a familiar nursery rhyme tune as a setting for a children's carol and 'Sing a song of Jesus' was born. However, its trial run was at our church's Christmas Sisterhood meeting, where it was performed by an enthusiastic group of mainly seventy and eighty-year-olds. They voted it a hit and it went on to take its place in 'Sound Bytes' as a piece for those at the youngest end of the age range. The Sisterhood were very flattered.

The tune SING A SONG OF SIXPENCE had to be adapted to fit a more regular metre, as the original is in an irregular pattern, although no one notices that when they are singing it with children. In addition, June Baker has included some delightful 'echo effects' to her new arrangement of the melody.

SING a song of Jesus, the baby in the hay.
We celebrate his birthday each year on Christmas Day.
His mother and his father looked down at him with joy,
so proud to be the parents of this special baby boy.

Sing a song of Jesus, the shepherds left their sheep.
The sound of angels' voices had wakened them from sleep.
Their song gave them the message a holy child was born
and so they ran to welcome him on that first Christmas morn.

Sing a song of Jesus, the wise men travelled far.
The winding way they followed was guided by a star.
They found the special baby their prophecies had told
and laid their gifts before him, frankincense and myrrh and gold.

Sing a song of Jesus, who grew to be a man
and told us in his stories how he became God's plan
to bring his love to people, his help and healing too
and show us by the way he lived, the things that we should do.

SING A SONG OF SIXPENCE (12 13.13 14.)

Traditional English
arranged June Baker (1936–)

Sing a song of Je - sus, the ba - by in the hay *the ba - by in the* hay. We ce - le-brate his birth - day each year on Christ-mas Day *each year on Christ-mas Day.* His moth - er and his fath - er looked down at him with joy, so proud to be the par - ents of this spe - cial ba - by boy. do.

POWER POLITICS

Herod must have been very shocked by that news of a new king, which the wise men brought to him inadvertently. But he may not have been too concerned about what he would do about the problem. Ruthlessness and self-preservation had kept him in power so far and all he had to do was wait for the men to report back and then he could take action.

The inner reflection in this piece follows his probable thought processes and sees him making his plans. But he would wait for their return in vain.

'THIS talk of kings is dangerous,' I muttered,
after the priests had left me and gone home.
'I have enough of trouble with the Romans
without a baby threatening my throne.

Those strange men seemed to know what they were seeking,
although they did not know just where to go.
When they return I'll question them more closely.
If they are right, I really need to know.

And if they are, then I must take precautions.
It would be wise to act within the hour.
And if some blood is spilt, then so it must be.
No Bethlehem child will undermine my power!

That lie of paying homage was a good one.
Who would suspect the motives of a king?
When they return I'll welcome them and feast them
and let them kneel and kiss my sovereign ring.

And then we'll talk of stars and tiny babies
and they will tell me all I want to hear.
They will not dream that he could be in danger
for I am Herod – what is there to fear?'

Lent and Easter

TURNING THE TABLES

Holy Week is an important time in any church and in the Methodist church that I attend we have a service each evening from Monday to Maundy Thursday and a morning service on Good Friday. As one of the Local Preachers, I have often been involved in this worship and it has resulted in a selection of material based around the events of that week.

'Turning the tables' is an attempt at looking at the uncharacteristic anger of Jesus from the point of view of those who bore the brunt of it – Caleb, a Temple trader; Daniel, a money changer; Gaius, a Gentile and Eliazar the priest. These pieces together make up a complete service of worship, but could also be used as individual characters at various points in Lent. The whole is best performed in the round and it is essential that a mess is made beforehand and no warning should be given to the congregation about the state of the church. Upturned tables and chairs, scattered receipt books, plastic money bags, coins, feathers and loose papers should be everywhere.

Open with the hymn 'We love the place, O God', although the irony may well be lost on many people, and continue with a rather conventional prayer. Then break the complacency with the following words:

> *'Apart from a few comments, you've all acted as if nothing has happened here. "It's all part of the event," you've said to yourselves. But what if it were for real? It has happened in some churches. Why destroy and desecrate a beautiful, holy place like this? Who would do such a thing? Who did do such a thing?'*

Then the four pieces are performed, each preceded by a different Gospel version of the story.

Caleb – Temple Trader (*Mark* 11:15–18)

You wouldn't believe it unless you'd seen it, but the man was absolutely mad. And nobody did anything about it. They just cowered against the walls and watched. I don't know where the police were, but they certainly didn't arrive in time to do anything. It was just absolute chaos and there was nothing you could do.

I suppose it just all happened so quickly. I mean, it was only an ordinary day. There was no warning of trouble – in fact, business was very good that day. There were masses of people milling around and you would have said that the general mood was excited and cheerful, until that man turned up. Passover week is always like that. Some people come to the Temple then that may never have been in Jerusalem before – and they're always in good spirits – and ready to spend.

My stall was set up in the usual place, just a little way in on the right hand side – I always say it's no use being too near the entrance, because people go past you before they know you're there. But by the time they get to where I am, they're starting to look round and that's the time when I try to catch their eye. I've always been noted for good merchandise – you ask anyone – 'you can't get a better pair of doves than from Caleb,' they'll say. And I charge a fair price. They're not cheap, I grant you. The only way to get a cheap pair of doves is if you bring them from home. But anybody who's got as far as the Temple before they think about buying doves for sacrifice has to recognise that it will cost them more. I have to pay more for them myself – and then it's certainly not cheap to have my stall pitched in that particular part of the courtyard – the Temple authorities must be coining it in! Then there are my other overheads, my own taxes, my profit margin – well, by the time you've worked all that out, you can easily justify my prices. Everybody knows that town-centre shopping is expensive – and if you're actually trading in the Temple ... well!

But that trading is perfectly legitimate. There was nothing wrong with what I was doing. The authorities were happy with it. It's been going on for years. And it doesn't stop people from worshipping in the inner courts of the Temple. I would have thought it was considered very convenient – having all the supplies on site, as it were – especially for those customers who live in the city itself. It was all going very well and I'd built up a very healthy business – until that maniac arrived.

He even took a whip to some people, you know! It was disgraceful. Throwing over the tables was bad enough. Two of the legs of my stall were totally smashed and as for the doves – well, I'll never see them again! But Jonathan, next door, was even worse. The end of the whip caught his cheek and I shouldn't think the scar will ever fully heal.

And that maniac, Jesus, had the nerve to be raging that it was his father's house and we'd made it a den of thieves and robbers. I don't know who his father is, but Jesus has certainly disgraced the family name.

I hope they lock him up and throw away the key – when they find him. Of course the temple police were not around when they were needed and only turned up when the villain had disappeared. But apparently he's known as one of those wandering teachers who's built up a large following, so it shouldn't be too difficult to track him down. According to all reports, he's only been known, up to now, for miracles of healing and telling good stories – oh, and having a go at the scribes and Pharisees with a few scathing comments – but then, who doesn't? But today in the Temple he was a real wild man – maybe he's just beginning to show his true colours.

As long as they catch him, that's all that matters to me – although I wouldn't mind a bit of compensation for loss of trade. But, in the meantime, I suppose I'd better find a carpenter who can make me some new table legs. Can you recommend anybody?

Daniel – Money Changer (*Matthew* 21:12–13)

WHAT the hell did that man think he was doing?

And what right had he to be there in the first place?

Can you see what he's done to my money? It's all over the place. I'll never get it all back – the thieves and vagabonds around here have already been in scavenging and because all my records are scattered all over the place, I'll never be able to find it all.

The villains are having a field day. They came pouring in as soon as they heard about the riot and they've been stuffing their pockets ever since.

It's outrageous!

I'd never even heard much about this 'Jesus' before – except for that extraordinary story that has been going round about the reformation of Zacchaeus the tax-collector.

Reformation, indeed! What did Zacchaeus need to reform from?

He was a legitimate government official – going about his regular business – raking in something on the side, of course, but that's just part of the job – and good luck to him, that's what I say.

He's no different to me. We charge a legitimate rate of interest. After all, you can't buy the money you need to use in the Temple from any other source than us money-changers, and everybody has to do it. You can't use your everyday coinage here.

So we are providing a service – and the interest we charge is only to keep us in business. Every business has to make a profit, or it doesn't last long.

So what's so different about being a trader in the Temple? You have to change your money somewhere – and where better than on holy ground? It puts money in the Temple coffers, so what's so wrong about it?

That man was out of his mind. All he's done is cause chaos and mayhem and lined the pockets of a few petty thieves. And left an enormous mess for somebody to clear up.

Why should he be allowed to disturb us like this? We've been going on this way for years and nobody has been too bothered about it before. What's wrong with my business? Money dealing is my way of life and always has been.

And as for calling this Temple precinct a den of thieves and robbers ...! Well, it may not have been before, but it is now. Look! There's another one after my coins!

Hey! Get away out of here! The Temple's no place for such as you!

Gaius – the Gentile (*Luke* 19:45–46)

I DON'T know who that man was, but I'm right behind everything that he did. This place has just become beyond a joke.

It's all right for the Jews themselves, they can go through all this chaos into the other courts of the Temple. Even the Jewish women are allowed to go into the next one, at least.

But for us Gentiles, this is the only part of the Temple that we *can* come into. 'The Court of the Gentiles' they call it – as if we were a separate breed from the rest of them.

But that man was right – they have made it into a den of thieves and robbers. Those money-changers are raking it in – they charge as much interest as they possibly can.

And the dove and animal sellers use the system to their own ends. They claim they are the only ones with animals pure enough to be sacrificed and they make sure that the examiners at the gate turn away any birds and animals that have been brought in from outside.

Talk about a monopoly on sales! They've got it made!

What's more, because of their exorbitant prices, even the mildest mannered people are ready to protest.

Add to that the sellers shouting their wares and the animal noises and the smells – I ask you, is this really a place of worship?

But, as Gentiles, we have no choice.

I suppose they just assume that Gentiles don't really come to worship – only to look at the sights.

Well, most do, I suppose. Especially at a time like the Passover when there's a lot going on and people are in a celebratory mood. The Jews certainly know how to party.

And there's something about their religion that intrigues me. After all, as a race they've had a lot of setbacks, but they still cling to this idea of only one God and one that will always see them through.

That's what keeps drawing me back to the Temple. I'm curious to know whether their God would accept me – and I'd love to find a quiet place here, where I could ask a question or two and sit and reflect. Maybe even pray.

There's been no chance of that recently and I don't think the Jews even considered how we Gentiles must have felt. They're too busy trading and arguing and trying to do each other down.

I wouldn't care so much, if it wasn't for the fact that they claim to be such religious people.

But there's no reverence here and not a chance of finding God. I'm sure they don't even realise how much their behaviour puts people off. After all, if you can't talk to God in their principal place of worship, where else are you going to find him?

But that seems to be their last consideration.

Maybe that man who charged in here and upset everything has some answers?

He was certainly very, very angry and was determined to make his point.

What's more, he seemed to have his priorities right and he was saying just what I felt. You'd have almost thought he was speaking for us Gentiles – which is very unusual for a Jew.

I'd like to see him given a chance to sort the place out properly, because he seemed to mean business and wasn't afraid of anybody.

Good for him, I say. I just hope it doesn't get him into too much trouble, but knowing the Temple authorities, I doubt if they'll let the matter lie.

But I hope he's shaken them up a bit – they certainly need to be.

Eliazar – the Priest (*John* 2:13–22)

THIS is the last straw. We cannot let this go on any longer.

We've let it go too far already.

We have watched this man wandering round the countryside, gathering his crowds and teaching and claiming to heal.

We've seen plenty like that before and usually they can be left to their own devices and contained within their own area – as long as we know what's going on.

But this Jesus always had a dangerous air about him – even as a young boy.

Apparently he was able to debate with the teachers here in the Temple and hold his own against them. There are one or two of our older colleagues who remember him clearly and say that he had a remarkable mind and was mature for his age.

After that incident we heard nothing from him for nearly twenty years – until he started his wandering ministry after being baptised by that wild prophet, John.

We started to smell a rat when he showed he was quite capable of giving clever answers to some of our trickiest questions.

He also began to be very subversive about some of our rules and regulations – claiming scriptural backing for his healing on the Sabbath and quoting King David when he was caught out eating ears of corn in the field – on the Sabbath again.

Then he started to speak out directly against us – warning people not to take too much notice of our outward piety – as if we were standing on street corners praying just to show off to the people!

A little publicity for the faith surely doesn't do any harm – and someone's got to do it.

But he called us hypocrites – two-faced – and insisted that our hearts weren't in our religion. He said people should look at our behaviour and judge for themselves – implying that we were saying one thing and doing another.

Who is he to judge?

But we've been insulted before. We're used to it – and we ignore most of it.

Nobody can be perfect – although we don't tell the people that, of course – we have to set them standards to live up to – and nobody knows what goes on behind our closed doors.

But what right has anyone to criticise us?

They don't know the responsibilities and strains of leadership – especially with people as volatile as ours – even with their so-called faith in God.

These last few weeks though, this Jesus has become dangerous.

We knew from our informants that he was determined to come to Jerusalem for the Passover and the combination of him and his followers and the Passover pilgrims was not a prospect to be savoured.

Then there came that procession into the city!

Now that really did set the alarm bells ringing. The crowd might not have realised the significance of him riding on a donkey, but we did.

He was setting the battle lines. This was a real challenge to our authority.

I still would not have thought that he would have the nerve to do what he did today.

We couldn't bar him from the Temple – it was his right to make a sacrifice.

We just kept an eye on him.

But nobody anticipated what he was going to do next – not even his followers.

He just seemed to suddenly blaze with anger and then stormed around with that whip, destroying everything and declaring it to be 'his father's house', not a den of robbers.

That 'father's house' claim cannot be tolerated.

It's another step on the road to him claiming to be the Messiah and it must end – before people really start believing him.

It's time for real action – but this time, on our part.

He must not be allowed to continue!

Andrew Pratt's hymn 'To bring a city to its sense' from *Whatever Name or Creed* (Stainer & Bell, 2002) fits in well at this point and the leader then continues:

> *Now let us sit quietly for five minutes – a long time, if you're not used to the silence.*
> *Look at the mess.*
> *Reflect on the characters you have heard.*
> *Remember that the only one to speak in favour of Jesus and to have a real longing for*
>   *worship was the Gentile – an outsider, not a Jew.*
>
> *Then think about the question:*
> *'How would Jesus react to what is going on in your church?*
> *Or in your life?'*
> *No one will be asked to give an answer.*
> *Just think honestly about it.*

End with prayers, Nick Fawcett's hymn 'Lord, we know that we have failed you' from *NewStart Hymns and Songs* (Kevin Mayhew, 1999) and a blessing.

GUILTY, OR NOT GUILTY?

Maundy Thursday is the day when people begin to feel guilty about betraying Jesus. Judas committed a deliberate act of betrayal with full knowledge of what he was doing. Peter was not brave enough to stand out against a crowd. The other disciples melted into the background. But there was one character who was a particularly reluctant player on the scene – Pilate. He tried to get out of making a decision and tried to make the crowd change its mind about their victim, but in the end he had to condemn Jesus to death. His hand-washing was a futile, but revealing, gesture, as he attempted to rid himself of the guilt of his verdict.

When we use the phrase, 'I wash my hands of the whole situation', are we echoing guilt at our own inability to influence attitudes for the good? This piece is intended to make us think carefully about our motives and attitudes; something we are constantly urged to do during the season of Lent.

Again it is best performed in the round, so that everyone can focus on the table (a low one is best), which is located centrally and on which are placed a cross, a clear glass bowl, a clear jug of clean water and a towel. It is ideally done with five different voices, but can be performed with fewer, if the roles are doubled up. The speakers should be dispersed around the circle, except for the two who perform the last piece – they should sit together. The order of readers is Pilate, Neighbour, Critic and Not Us!

When Pilate has finished speaking, the second reader from Not Us! moves forward to the table, pours the water from the jug into the bowl, then takes it and the towel over to Pilate, who washes his hands (no soap) and dries them. The bowl and towel are placed back on the table. When the Neighbour has finished speaking, it is Pilate who offers the bowl. For the Critic, it is the Neighbour and for the Not Us! couple it is the Critic. This way each speaker is linked to the guilt, which is why the performance will be more effective with five people.

When the last couple have finished speaking and washed their hands, the bowl is placed on the table. It will be seen that the water has changed colour. After a pause for reflection the leader of worship moves forward and lifts the bowl so that all can see it. Then these words can be used, or the leader can respond with personal reflections on what has happened.

'We have listened to what these people have had to say about themselves and, no doubt, in our own minds we have made judgements about them. Guilty, or not guilty! Each of them came here with clean hands and, because they were able to justify themselves in their own eyes, they washed their hands free of guilt.

Their hands were clean, but the water is now dirty. What does that mean?

And what would happen if we each washed our hands in the same water? We know that it would only deepen the colour. Are our hands ever really clean?'

It may not be appropriate for every group, but perhaps after a period of silent reflection some people from the group may also wish to wash their hands in the bowl, as a sign of penitence. The worship would end most appropriately with reflective music, or 'When I survey the wondrous cross', sung quietly.

Pilate

I WAS uneasy about this whole case from the start. Nothing was right about it and the Jews are such devious people to deal with – well, their leaders are anyway – and they have their own means of getting the crowd on their side.

It was inevitable that something like this would happen here. My friends warned me when I was given the job, but once I was appointed I couldn't very well refuse, could I?

But I was warned that the Jewish religion was a tricky one to handle and I know to my cost that it's true.

So when they brought this wandering teacher in, it was bound to mean trouble. If the Sadducees and the Pharisees and the High Priest were all already against him, then what chance did he have?

The charges they brought against him didn't seem to mean a great deal. They said he claimed to be a king – which was supposed to put me on my guard in defence of the Emperor – but Jesus said himself that he wasn't intending to be that kind of a king and then started talking about other worlds and heaven. That seemed quite harmless to me – deluded, but harmless.

But somewhere in the middle of my questioning I was sent an urgent message from my wife, warning me to have nothing to do with the case. Now this really did make me feel uneasy. She doesn't normally have any interest at all in my official hearings – she knows it's none of her business – so this was very different.

Apparently she'd had a frightening dream about this man Jesus – and she'd been so alarmed that she'd taken it very seriously.

I would have ignored it, but I was struck by the note of fear in her message. She is unhappy here, I know. She misses her family and friends and her social life. No one here has taken on Roman ways, except Herod, and he hadn't made us feel welcome at all. So I've been used to her complaints about everything and her constant wish to get back to real civilisation – but I've never known her to be so agitated about one of my cases with a particular Jew before. Perhaps she realised that in this case I held the power of life and death, although it's not the first time. Maybe her servants had been pleading for the man. He seems very popular with such people. But whatever the source of the message, it slightly alarmed me and made me anxious to get the case off my hands.

It was then that somebody mentioned that Jesus was a Galilean and I thought I had the answer. Send him to Herod! He was in Jerusalem – let him deal with it. The priests and the lawyers wouldn't be happy about it, but they had no choice, and I thought that would be the last I would see of them that day.

Herod didn't do anything at all! I shouldn't have expected that he would. All he ever wanted was to be entertained and to keep himself out of harm's way. But he didn't get the entertainment, because Jesus didn't speak a word, so Herod dressed him up for his own amusement and then sent him back to me.

We talked it over later that day – Herod and I – and we knew we'd both been manipulated, but what could we have done? That was the first time that I realised that he and I might be able to get on with each other after all.

But his attitude didn't solve my problem. The priests and lawyers were still baying for the Galilean's blood and by now they had stirred the crowd up, so that they were also demanding his crucifixion. I did have one more trick up my sleeve. The Jews' own custom was to have a prisoner of their choice released at the Feast of the Passover and I thought I might just be able to persuade them to release Jesus. I was only half right. They did want Jesus released, but not my prisoner. It was another Jesus they were shouting for – Bar Abbas, Jesus Bar Abbas – a notorious villain if ever there was one. If there were those in the crowd who were shouting for Jesus of Nazareth, their cries were being twisted to sound like something else, or drowned out altogether.

I tried – I really tried to persuade that crowd – but it wasn't a crowd, by this time it was a mob. And they wanted blood. The blood of Jesus the Galilean.

In the end I gave in. There would have been a riot otherwise and many innocent people would have been hurt, or killed.

So Jesus became a sacrifice – and the strange thing was – he didn't fight it!

But I will not take the blame upon myself. I tried hard to do something about it, but I was overwhelmed by circumstances. They were to blame – and the priests and the lawyers and the ones in the crowd who were really against him. They stirred up that uncontrollable mob, not me!

Which is why I took the basin and the towel and – where everyone could see – I washed my hands of the whole case.

My wife was pleased, but I can't forget what I have done – it haunts me. I can't wash his blood from my hands with water. I wish there was some way that I could.

Neighbour *(based on a true case)*

You'd never believe it if I told you what my neighbours do to their children. I don't think they're being deliberately cruel, you understand. But, it's just ...

Well, I know they both work very hard. They have to, to keep body and soul together. They already had the little girl when they moved in next door and you could tell they didn't have much money when you saw the few tatty bits and pieces of furniture they brought with them. It wasn't very long after that when I saw she was pregnant again – she may have worn loose clothes, but I could tell why she was doing it. She carried on working though, so did he. He was on nights; she worked days in the local shop. They must have hardly seen each other – in fact, it makes you wonder how ... well, never mind!

Then, when she had the new baby, she lost her job and was at home all the time. In fact, that was when I first starting speaking to her – when I saw her coming past my door with the baby in her arms and the little girl trailing behind. Well, you have to say something about a new baby, don't you?

We spoke once or twice after that. In fact, I was beginning to think she was quite nice, until that day she told me she'd got a new job. I was pleased for her – until she told me it would mean her working nights as well as her husband.

'What are you going to do about the children?' I asked her.

'Oh, they'll be all right!' she said. 'The baby sleeps right through and I'll make sure the little girl can't wander out of the bedroom until I get back.'

I just stared at her. 'What do you mean?'

'Well, I've got one of those strap things you use to keep hold of a child when you're out with them. You know, one end fastens to their wrist and the other to yours. I'll just fasten one end on her wrist and the other to the bed, then she'll be safe.' Just then the baby started crying and off she went.

And that's what they're doing. I see them go off each night – she goes first, he goes an hour later and she gets back about two in the morning. I hear her coming up the street and opening and shutting the door. And all I can think of is those poor kids left on their own – one of them tied to the bed.

But what can I do? It's none of my business! My friend says I should report them to the NSPCC, but I can't do that. They would know who it was that had done it. And I'm not offering to look after the kids either – that's their problem, not mine. Surely they've got some family or friends – let them sort it out. I really do think something ought to be done. But it's nothing to do with me!

Critic *(Pauses should be made between each complaint)*

Isn't it disgraceful how people these days don't seem to care about the church any more? The only time you hear them saying the names of God and Christ, they're using them as swear words. And some people have never seen the inside of a church unless they've been to a wedding or a funeral – and most of them don't take place in church any more.

I blame the schools. When we were at school we were taught all about the Bible and Jesus – even if some of the teachers weren't very good at it. But we were taught to sing hymns and to learn the Ten Commandments and how to say the Lord's Prayer – and they don't get that kind of thing in schools today.

And we were sent to Sunday School as well. I remember we had to learn a verse from the Bible every week and, if we could remember it, we got a sticker with a Bible picture on it. There was always a competition to see who got the most.

Most children these days don't even come to Sunday School – or Junior Church, or whatever newfangled name they call it. Some of them go to Scouts, or Guides, or one of those things, but they evidently don't teach them much about church there either. You can tell that by the way they behave on the odd occasion they do turn up for special services. But you can't get the right people to run these things – not even the Sunday School. Nobody seems to want to make any kind of commitment. They can't do – they're always appealing for more people to help out.

But the parents don't help at all. Young parents these days always seem to have so much to do. Going to church isn't one of their priorities – oh, no! They're far more likely to be at the supermarket, or watching football, or taking the children out for the day. They don't seem to want to give their children any lasting values. Everything has to be bright and new and entertaining. They can't see how much comfort there is in doing things in the old-fashioned ways.

The Minister doesn't help either. Always trotting off to do school assemblies and charity meetings and sending other people to visit instead of coming himself. He should be concentrating more on his preaching – some of the Ministers in my younger days used to draw crowds of folk to church to listen. It doesn't happen very often now.

But there's nothing I can do about it. It's not my fault if people don't want to know. I've lived a good life, as far as I can, and as long as the church lasts out for my lifetime, that's all that matters.

Not Us! (*details in these pieces can be changed, as appropriate*)

One   WE inherited the problem –

Two   – said the NCB when they took over the coal tips at Aberfan.

One   It's all a matter of economics –

Two   – say the multi-national companies destroying the rainforests.

One   It's political and part of our history –

Two   – say warring factions all over the globe.

One   We don't make people buy –

Two   – say the drug barons.

One   We don't expect people to do this in real life –

Two   – say the makers of violent or pornographic films.

Pause

One   We're giving people what they want –

Two   – say the brewers – to the family of an alcoholic.

One   We're giving people what they want –

Two   – say the tobacco firms – to a victim of lung cancer.

One   We're giving people what they want –

Two   – say the lottery organisers – to the family of a mother who never has enough money for food.

One   We're giving people what they want –

Two   – say the credit card companies – to the families who are never out of debt.

Together   It's not our problem!

JESUS THE CARPENTER

As one who was born and bred in northern working class England, I suffer occasional bouts of intense irritation with certain southerners, who should know better than to look down their noses at me simply because my vowel sounds are different to their own. Would they have done the same to Jesus? He came from a northern working class home too. There is plenty of evidence in the gospels that Jesus suffered from ridicule in certain quarters because of his accent and his down-to-earth way of teaching. He was only a carpenter's son, after all.

There are parts of the church today where you could be forgiven for forgetting that fact. Jesus has been portrayed as middle class and educated, because that is the picture which is most comfortable for many Christians. But it bears little resemblance to the everyday ministry of Christ in his time. He did not ignore the rich, but had difficulty in getting through to them. He had his worst problems with the intellectual religious officials who were too superior for their own good and hypocritical about their own lifestyles, whilst at the same time demanding unattainable standards of the people they should have been serving.

Jesus, the carpenter, understood the ways, the thinking, the pressures, the problems and the relationship with God of everyday working folk. He had been brought up as a craftsman, learning to work with his hands and earn a living to help to support his family. Many of his stories were told from this background and he had a rapport with ordinary people, which was why they flocked around him. He reached out to touch them with his hands and his heart.

When we put this carpenter into a different social class we automatically alienate a whole range of the ordinary folk whom Jesus dealt with day by day. Jesus worked with wood, had rough hands and spoke the local language with a northern accent. This song/hymn is an attempt to bring Jesus down to earth again. It was originally written to the tune BLOW THE WIND SOUTHERLY.

Jesus the carpenter, hanging on Calvary,
nails through your feet and your work-hardened hands –
wood you have worked with and wood is your destiny –
paying the price of our sinful demands.

You came to our world as a part of a family,
living and learning the carpenter's trade.
You followed your father's instructions so faithfully,
shaping and crafting the yokes that you made:
Chorus

You called other workmen to join in your ministry,
laying rough hands on the sick and the lame.
You taught of God's love with such power and authority,
people who knew you believed you insane:
Chorus

You faced with great courage the open hostility
coming from those who believed they were right.
They stripped you and beat you and laughed at you finally,
thinking your death was the end of the fight:
Chorus

But we, who now know that you ended triumphantly
working with wood till your task was complete,
can come to your cross with our hope and humility,
laying our pride at the carpenter's feet:
Chorus

BLOW THE WIND SOUTHERLY   *Traditional English*
(13.10.13.10. and Chorus)   *arranged Paul Bateman (1954–)*

came to our world as a part of a fa - mil - y,

liv - ing and learn - ing the car - pen - ter's trade. You

fol - lowed your fa - ther's in - struc - tions so faith - ful - ly,

D.C.

shap - ing and craft - ing the yokes that you made:

LOVE UNKNOWN

Not everyone is used to praying with their eyes open, unless perhaps they are focussing on a candle or a cross. This piece was written as a visual prayer with tools of the carpenter's trade lying around and wooden objects ranging from chairs to carvings, including one in which the fault had been incorporated into the carved dish to make it a thing of beauty. The people were asked to keep their eyes open and the tools and objects were shown around at the appropriate time. This prayer was written for the same service as 'Jesus the carpenter'.

LOVE unknown, Lord, how could you do it?
Coming from the glory of the Father to a carpenter's workshop in Nazareth?
Taking on the ordinary, the everyday, the working life?

And yet, in choosing the life of a carpenter, you chose well.

Carpenters working with wood can shape it and cut it down to size and make it right for its purpose.

Carpenters can smooth rough edges and make joints that dovetail and shave off the corners of square pegs so that they *can* fit into round holes.

And in their spare time they can work with the wood and the grain to make objects of pleasure and beauty – even including the flaws.

Carpentry was the right choice for you.

Jesus the carpenter, take us in hand and shape us.
Plane our rough edges, transform our faults and flaws and make us fit for your purpose.

Work on us Lord, and help us to work with you, so that what we create together will be strong and useful.

And when we face the crosses we all must bear in life – knowing, as you did, that there is nothing we can do to change the situation – let us remember your strong workman's hands were useless against the nails – but you faced it and went through it.

Christ the carpenter, we draw our strength from you.

PRAYER FOR GOOD FRIDAY

A prayer to open worship on this very significant day.

WE come here today to remember a special, but tragic, day in our Christian calendar.
On this day we look at the cross, not just as a symbol of our faith, but also as an instrument of torture and death.

Today is a solemn, sobering day, Lord – a very sombre day in the calendar of the events of your life.

On this day we remember that you reaped the rewards of being controversial in your attitude to religious bigotry.

On this day we see the betrayal of friendship and its consequences.

On this day we remember that your enemies appear to have got the upper hand.

On this day we remember that all the prophecies about your end were justified.

On this day we see the casual cruelty of Roman authority and execution.

On this day we see how unreliable your followers proved to be in a real crisis.

On this day we appeared to see the death of God.

Be with us, Lord, as we reflect on this day and the effect that it has on our lives.

Help us to remember that religious bigotry, cruelty and unreliability are still a part of our everyday lives and that enemies of the faith still surround us.

Show us how we can learn from your example of suffering that you were prepared to go to any lengths to prove just how much God cares about his people.

Then help us to translate all that we learn into loving actions and reactions to the people around us who need that sacrificial love.

Otherwise your cross would have been in vain.

JESUS IN THE GARDEN WEEPING

Throughout the period of the arrest, trial, crucifixion and resurrection of Jesus, the disciples were bewildered, frightened, shocked and ashamed and had entirely forgotten his promise that death would not be the end for him. This hymn contains some of those emotions and the reassurance that we need from Jesus ourselves, when events shake our own faith.

JESUS in the garden weeping,
on the ground disciples sleeping,
through the night the soldiers creeping –
Judas leading all the way.

Jesus, his accusers facing,
in the courtyard Peter pacing,
full of fear, his heart is racing –
in his weakness, he'll betray.

Jesus on the cross now dying,
at his feet his mother crying,
John, alone, his help supplying –
in the shadows women pray.

Jesus in the garden risen,
proving death was not his prison.
Mary saw the angel vision –
'Do not seek him here today.'

Jesus in that room appearing
to his friends, their spirits cheering.
'Peace be with you,' in their hearing
drove their guilty fear away.

Jesus, when we are mistaken,
when our hold on faith is shaken,
grant forgiveness, Lord, awaken
us to Easter hope this day.

EDMUND (8 8 8.7.) *Colin Nicholson (1932–)*

Je - sus in the gar - den weep-ing,— on the ground dis - ci - ples sleep-ing,— through the night the sol - diers creep-ing – Ju - das lead - ing all the way.

hope this day, Eas - ter hope this day.

THE MORNING AFTER

How can we ever really imagine the devastation felt by those disciples on this in-between day? We know that they had nothing to fear. We see that Jesus fulfilled his promise of resurrection and we cannot forget that. But they did not have the benefit of our hindsight. History had not taken that giant leap forward for them. All they knew was that life would never be the same again, but they believed that they would have to live it now without their friend and leader. The worst had happened and they could not know that it would only be for a day.

One   ON THE second day the crowds were Sabbath-solemn and minding their own business.

Two   On the second day Judas committed suicide because he could not forgive himself.

One   On the second day Herod threw a party because no one could blame him for anything.

Two   On the second day Pilate smiled to himself because his wife was wrong – for once!

One   On the second day the High Priest felt he could relax because he'd spent his money well.

Two   On the second day the Pharisees and Sadducees congratulated each other that it was all over.

One   On the second day the disciples locked the doors and planned their journeys home.

Two   On the second day Peter knew he'd spoken out once too often and there was nothing he could do.

One   On the second day Mary and the other women wept and wept and then prepared their spices.

Two   On the second day the soldiers guarded the sealed grave and wondered why they bothered.

Three   And on the third day Jesus said, 'What did I tell you?'

Pentecost

PENTECOST

From fear of failure to instant success. From closed shutters to open spaces. From frightened whispers to confident proclamation. What a difference a day made.

Pentecost that year changed everything and made the followers into leaders fired with enthusiasm and filled with power. Our prayer is that we can follow their example.

Lord, your first followers shut themselves tightly into a room to wait for the
  coming of your Spirit.
They were afraid of mockery, of persecution and the danger of having to follow
  you to the cross.

But when your Spirit came, the wind was strong and blew away their doubts.
It refreshed and invigorated them.
It blew them out of their locked room.

The fire of your Spirit rested on their heads, to confirm their commitment and
blazed in their hearts to set them alight for you.

So, driven by the wind and lit by the fire, they spilled out into the world to speak
the languages of your love.

Dear God, so often we confine ourselves within four walls because we are so
afraid of the world outside.

We hear your call to follow in the footsteps of Jesus, but we are not sure we can go
so far.

Break through into our lives with your cleansing, driving wind and help us to be
willing to be carried along in that power, outside the confines of our safe and
secure walls.

Fire our hearts again with the flame of your love; so that we may have a burning
desire to reach out to others in your name.

Teach us the language of love that confirms our knowledge of you and speaks to
the hearts of all the peoples of your family.

Come, Holy Spirit, come.
Change us and set us free.

ENERGY

What – or who – made these people different? How did they feel? Did they understand
their experience? How did they explain it later?
   What happens when the Holy Spirit fills someone?

ENERGY!
From that Pentecost day.
Pure, unadulterated energy.

The sound of driving wind
bent us to our knees.
We could not stand against it.

The flames burned light and heat
into a coronet of confirmation.

We could not be quiet.
We were babbling
and bubbling over with words and news.
No wonder they assumed
that we were drunk.

We felt it too.

Drunk with energy,
enthusiasm and power –
after bewildering days
when stories circled
and doubt curled round their edges.
We had not known, as we gathered,
what to expect.
Liberation was so swift.

But now,
we really can do anything,
not just by name,
but also with his power.

He has returned
as Spirit burning and burdening our hearts.

Pentecost has new dimensions now.

Energy!
Driving energy!

INSPIRATION

Although it is possible to sing with great feeling and to ask for the Spirit to sweep through the church, it is also very easy to feel dispirited about that same church and our own Christian experience. If there is no sound of rushing wind, or tongues of fire, or even energy that seems to be sustaining us, then we must look again at the origins of the word 'spirit' and perhaps remember the words of the old hymn, 'Breathe on me, breath of God.' Which led me to think of balloons – not the most well-known symbol associated with Pentecost!

I HATE balloons!
Ever since that day
one horrid child
burst one behind me
at a party,
when I was only four,
or thereabouts –
I've hated balloons.

And yet ...

a street-seller
captivates children –
and me –
by making shapes and animals,
as he breathes life
into long, thin balloons
and curves and twists them
in his hands.
Then, suddenly, a dog!
And a delighted child
sees, not breath encased,
only a new friend
to carry home with glee.

Empty,
balloons are nothing.
Air-filled,
they live.

Come Holy Spirit,
pour new life into me,
that I may fill
and change
and live and grow,
transformed
by the very breath of God.

WIND OF THE SPIRIT

Sometimes a tune gets lodged in the brain and will not shift until new words are written for it. Why it had to be the tune to 'God rest you merry, gentlemen' is a bit of a mystery, except that it is a good, happy tune to sing. But from Christmas to Pentecost is a long time for that irritant factor to last, until suddenly the words of the chorus were triggered by the reflection that the pilgrim church seemed to spend far too much time resting at the side of the road, rather than moving on. We had probably been singing Sydney Carter's 'One more step along the world I go' again.

Pentecost is a real gift for three-point-sermon preachers and equally good for hymn writers – one verse each for wind, fire and tongues and a closing verse containing all three. So the pattern was set. The hymn was first published in 'Worship Live' with the usual suggestion to composers that they may like to try writing a new tune. One of these tunes – not Ian Sharp's! – was sent with the comment that perhaps the words 'blow off the cobwebs of the past' were too strong to be sung by an elderly, conventional congregation. A clear case of missing the point.

WIND of the Spirit, move us on,
drive us before your force.
We need that power to strengthen us
of which you are the source.
Blow off the cobwebs of the past
and set us on your course:
O come Holy Spirit, move us on, move us on.
O come Holy Spirit, move us on.

Fire of the Spirit, burn in us,
surround us with your light.
Destroy our sense of apathy,
give us the will to fight.
That with our hearts on fire for Christ
we set the world alight:
Chorus

Voice of the Spirit speak to us,
give us your words to say.
Inspire the language of your love,
help us to preach and pray.
That all may hear of saving grace
translated for their day:
Chorus

Christ, let your Spirit sweep through us,
your serving church renew.
Give us new hope and confidence
in all the work we do.
That those who seek for faith today
may find their way to you:
Chorus

GOD REST YOU MERRY (8.6.8.6.8.6. and Chorus)

Traditional English
arranged Ian Sharp (1943–)

The Biblical Way

The Bible is a wonderful yet strange book. Where else would you find history and song rubbing shoulders, except perhaps in an encyclopaedia? The Bible contains stimulating teaching, but it stands alongside records of atrocities committed in the name of religion. Almost all of the people within its pages have faults and foibles and constantly have to be told by God to get back on the right track. There are inspired visions and dismal failures; giant figures of faith with feet of clay; political conflicts and religious rituals. Texts can be found and made to fit any viewpoint taken by anyone on any subject.

Yet the Bible is the basic textbook of our faith and although it is challenging, it is also very reassuring. The people within its pages were characters just like us and it is so good to know that we do not have to be perfect to be chosen by God. In fact, if we did think ourselves perfect, then we wouldn't be of any use to God. That was a lesson that certain religious authoritarian figures had to learn from Jesus.

Relating to God through the Bible becomes a personal search for our own lessons and links. This section contains some of the characters and teachings that have helped me on my biblical way.

THE BIBLE IS FULL OF ADVENTURES OF FAITH

WHATEVER I DO, YOU CAN DO, GOD SAID   *Graham Wilkinson (1958–)*
(11.8.11.8. and Chorus)

The Bi-ble is full of ad-ven-tures of faith of peo-ple who fol-lowed God's
call;_____ from Ab-ram and Mo-ses to Pe-ter and John, from
Sam-uel and Da-vid to Paul. 'What-ev-er I do, you can
do,' God said. 'Wher-ev-er I go, you can fol-low._____
*Power will be gi-ven for your work to-day, if you trust in me for to-mor-row.'_*

THE BIBLE is full of adventures of faith
of people who followed God's call;
from Abram and Moses to Peter and John,
from Samuel and David to Paul.
'Whatever I do, you can do,' God said.
'Wherever I go, you can follow.
Power will be given for your work today,
if you trust in me for tomorrow.'

Now Abram was old and was settled in life
and Samuel was only a boy,
but when the Lord called them they did not hold back –
they answered his challenge with joy.
Chorus

King David was called when a young shepherd lad.
Paul was an intelligent man.
And Moses was very reluctant to go,
but all played a part in God's plan.
Chorus

God's plans for the future are all in our hands,
whatever our age, shape, or size.
Lord, help us to follow wherever you lead –
to look at the world through your eyes.
Chorus

Graham Wilkinson was once a member of the youth fellowship that met in our home. He started to play the organ at church as soon as his legs were long enough for his feet to reach the pedals. When he married he moved to another church in our Circuit. The building was very dilapidated, but in a good position on a main road site. Eventually the largely elderly congregation took the brave decision to demolish the old building and replace it with a new one. This was a huge financial commitment for them, but they believed that God was encouraging them to go ahead with the project and many covenants of money were made and much fundraising lay ahead of them.

At this point, Graham asked me to write a hymn for them, which could become almost a 'theme tune' to their efforts. It had to be suitable for all ages; it must have a chorus and he asked that it should not be set to a known tune, as he wanted to compose a suitable tune for it himself. That final request was the most difficult to fulfil. I cannot write, read, or play music. It is a foreign language to me. I don't even sing very well. But I have a strong sense of rhythm, rhyme and metre and can hold a tune in my head easily. This is how I write my hymns and songs. To be asked to do that without a tune proved to be almost impossible, but not quite.

This piece has an unusual metre, to say the least, and presented Graham with quite a challenge. The whole piece was included in 'Sound Bytes' in 1999.

EVE

When I submitted the previous piece to Janet Wootton, the editor of 'Worship Live', she pointed out that it only contained male characters from the Bible as examples of people of faith. My reasons for doing this were quite simply based on familiarity. That song was written with children in mind and the characters chosen were people they may have already heard about, although that is not necessarily the case today. Of course, as we saw in Advent, there are prominent female biblical characters, but they are not always so well known as to be instantly recognisable. This is a disappointment to many feminists and they are working hard to correct the balance.

I am not really a feminist – in spite of what my husband may say to the contrary. My belief is in people – male, female, young, old, black, white, or any other colour. Jesus treated everyone with equal attention and we should follow that example.

So I could not be entirely serious when someone else challenged me to write a hymn on Eve as the 'token woman' – an impossible subject to tackle in this way, and one thrown at me only to provoke some kind of indignant reaction – unsuccessfully, as it turned out! This tongue-in-cheek offering was the result. It has been set to music, which was a great surprise to me, and I think I would despair if anyone seriously attempted to use it as a congregational hymn. It is a piece of irony with a tune – and not intended to offend anyone!

It may be at this point that more serious readers will wonder about the wisdom of reading further. Please don't stop!

EVE   June Baker (1936–)

In Ed-en's ear-ly___ gold-en days when bees first start-ed___ hum-min'– who had to face the ser-pent's___ tongue and be the first one in___ the___ wrong? Poor Eve, the tok-en

In Eden's early golden days
when bees first started hummin' –
who had to face the serpent's tongue
and be the first one in the wrong?
Poor Eve, the token woman.

And when we meet at heaven's gate
and hear the harp strings strummin' –
a lonely soul will greet us there,
with scarlet ribbons in her hair
and say in tones of deep despair,
'I'm Eve, the token woman.'

YOU'RE NEVER TOO OLD

God challenges us to do the strangest things sometimes. The earliest Bible chapters are full of such stories and Abraham and Sarah had incident-filled lives because of their commitment to God. It is intriguing to imagine how some of their neighbours must have reacted to the events.

Martha and Miriam here echo the comedian Les Dawson's famous duo with Roy Barraclough, Cissie and Ada. It is not just the words that matter. There is also much nudging and winking and gestures of 'you know what I mean, don't you?' Normal, gossipy conversation of the kind Christians would never engage in, would we?

Local gossip is as old as the hills. These two participants have stepped out of the background of *Genesis* 12. Named Martha and Miriam, they could equally be Enoch and Eli. Men gossip too! I have used the familiar Abraham and Sarah names, even though I realise this is not strictly correct, but 'Abram' and 'Sarai' seemed clumsy in speech. Purists can change them if they wish!

Martha: Here, have you heard the latest?

Miriam: What's that then?

Martha: Well, you know that couple that live next door to me?

Miriam: Which side?

Martha: Nearest to the well – they moved in not long after they were married. Came from Ur with his father years ago.

Miriam: Who's 'er with his father? I never knew he was involved with a woman. You are talking about that old fellow Terah – died a few years back? Did he really have another woman? Well I never!

Martha: No, you fool! Ur – U-R, that place in Babylonia! Oooh you do get the wrong end of a story!

Miriam: Sorry!

Martha: The one I'm talking about is Abraham. His wife's that nice woman – Sarah.

Miriam: Oh! Yes! The one who can't have ...

Martha: ... children. That's right!

Miriam: OK. I've got you. Well, what about them then?

Martha: How old do you think he is?

Miriam: Er ... looks about sixty, I would say. But you can't really tell with that beard.

Martha: Well, he's seventy-five if he's a day.

Miriam: Is he? Well, I suppose he must be. His father, the one I thought you said had another woman, he was the same age as my grandmother. Always thought he fancied her, you know. Which is why when you said Ur, I thought you meant ...

Martha: *(interrupting)* Are you going to let me finish my story?

Miriam: Sorry! I was just ...

Martha: *(interrupting again)* This Abraham – he's definitely seventy-five years old, but do you know what he's going to do?

Miriam: No! But I think you're going to tell me.

Martha: He's uprooting his whole family and he's off to find a new land.

Miriam: Well, that's not all that strange – everybody's a bit of a nomad these days.

Martha: Will you listen! He's only doing it because he reckons him upstairs is telling him to go.

Miriam: You mean the landlord? I wouldn't have thought Abraham would have been the type to get behind with the rent.

Martha: No, you idiot! Not the landlord! God!

Miriam: God! Oooh ... sorry!

Martha: Yes, God! Sarah was telling me this morning. She says he's suddenly got this idea fixed in his head about them moving on and he insists it was God who told him to do it.

Miriam: Silly old fool! You'd think he'd know better.

Martha: Unless he's getting a bit ... confused, of course!

Miriam: Yes. My Grandma used to hear voices.

Martha: Anyway, they're going. They started packing this morning. Apparently if God says go, they go.

Miriam: Well, I wouldn't start travelling again at that age – not that I am, of course!

Martha: Hm! Sarah certainly wasn't too pleased about it. She thinks Abraham says a lot of this stuff off the top of his head. She doesn't think God is all that interested in them. I suppose you wouldn't in her position.

Miriam: You mean her not being able ...

Martha: ... to have children – yes.

Miriam: Well, who knows? If they are moving on again at their age, just because they believe God is telling them to do it – maybe a change of air will do her good in that respect as well.

Martha: What? You mean a baby? Don't be so daft – she's far too old.

Miriam: Ah, yes! But what if God told them it would happen? Once you start believing in that kind of thing you never know what will happen next!

Martha: I know! But there are limits ... aren't there?

A LION'S TALE

This piece might be called a 'liberal interpretation' of a Bible story and should not be read by anyone who believes that the Bible is, solely, a very serious collection of books that should always be treated in a scholarly manner. All my life I have written pieces for performance – monologues, we used to call them. Many of these were written for church social events and were crammed with 'in-jokes' and references to specific people. They were doggerel at its best, or worst, depending on your opinion of such material. Certainly they were always written for a small local audience and usually in the style of the famous 'Albert and the Lion' pieces.

This one has a more universal appeal, as it is a Bible story, although you may never have heard it told like this before. It is best read aloud and children of all ages up to ninety and beyond have been happy to listen to it. Have fun!

WELL, hello there, I'm Leo the lion –
the king of the jungle, that's me.
I'm big and I'm strong and I'm healthy
and I eat lots of meat for my tea.

I used to live out in wild places
where the deer and the antelope roam,
with the stars up above for a ceiling
and a shady old tree for my home.

Of course, that's all right when it's sunny,
but it does get quite wet when it rains
and even though that's not too often
it sets off the old aches and pains.

So when last year the hunters went searching
I decided I'd not run too fast,
after so many years in the open
there was chance for a warm den at last.

And what a safe haven I landed –
behind the king's palace, no less –
with meals and companions provided,
my capture seemed quite a success.

The den it was high, wide and handsome,
with meat supplies constantly brought.
They were fresh, they were lean, they were tender –
more important – they needn't be caught!

There were one great big lion named Wallace,
his nose were all covered in scars
and he lay in a somnolent posture
with the side of his face 'neath the bars.

No there wasn't. I'm telling a lie now.
He's part of the future, you'll see.
One day he'll be meeting his Albert
at some place called Blackpool, on sea.

So let us get back to this story.
As I said, I was caught by the king
and taken to live near the palace
and taught to walk round in a ring.

I soon became used to this lifestyle.
It was warm and protected – and more,
there were regular mealtimes provided,
so I really had no need to roar.

There didn't seem much aim or purpose
and I soon got to snoozing all day,
'cos I didn't yet know for this comfort
there was one price expected to pay.

The day that I started to wonder
was the first day that I missed my food.
I couldn't think what might have happened.
Was the keeper not feeling too good?

I really was starting to worry
when the next day again saw no meat,
they must know that I can get quite angry
if there's nothing brought for me to eat.

On the third day the keeper came looking,
but brought me no meal – not a crust!
So to show him just how I was feeling
I started to roar fit to bust.

As I was a-roaring and shouting
I saw the king shaking with fright
and then heard him say to the keeper,
'It seems that you've got them just right.'

Then they left us alone till the evening
and by then we were all in a state
of roaring and pacing and fighting –
when we heard someone open the gate.

We all stopped to watch what was happening
and were ready to pounce any minute,
especially if someone had brought us
a cart with a fresh meal piled in it.

But there in the doorway a man stood
with others, who pushed him right in,
saying, 'Sort that lot out, if you can, Dan.
I bet that's one fight you can't win.'

Well, by this time we all were so hungry
we'd have killed for some baked beans and chips!
And to see that man stand there so helpless,
it soon had us licking our lips.

We began moving hungrily forward
with menace, 'cos that is our way,
and were just getting to striking distance
when he suddenly knelt down to pray.

'Twere a proper setback for us lions.
That isn't the way it should be.
When ordinary folk see us coming
they usually turn round and flee.

But this man, whose friends called him Daniel,
was surely decidedly odd.
Instead of being frightened of lions,
he only respected his God.

But even a lion has scruples,
so I said to the rest of the pride,
'It wouldn't be right to kill this one.
He's so brave, he won't even hide.'

The rest of the lions consented
and decided to wait for their food,
'cos they reckoned with all of that praying
his bony knees wouldn't taste good.

When Dan's enemies came out to fetch him,
at least to pick up any bones,
they couldn't believe he was still there
and from then spoke of him in hushed tones.

Now we lions were not much in favour,
'cos we shouldn't have left him alone.
But they won't put us back in the desert,
though they are sending us on to Rome.

There's talk of a huge Coliseum
and fighting with soldiers and such.
I don't think that we older lions
will like to do that very much.

But, if those of a new generation
are starved until they're near defeat,
I wonder what decadent Romans
will throw to those lions to eat?

PERSISTENT GOD

There is no retirement age for Christians. That may be good or bad news, depending on your age or attitude to life at the time of reading. But it is a fact. Look at the characters in the Bible, particularly in the Old Testament, and recognise how many of them would have been unemployable in today's youth-centred working environment.

Yet God calls on the wisdom and trust of these elderly people to make a significant difference in the lives of many others.

So, forget about retirement – God's work lasts a lifetime.

PERSISTENT God,
you are no respecter of old age
and you never have been.
You called so many people
long after others had assumed their useful lives were over.

Abraham was asked to move to a new country and take on a new name.
Sarah had her child long after it was thought possible.
Moses grew tetchy and weary leading rebellious people on a wilderness journey.
Elizabeth was far too old to be the mother of John the Baptist,
but that didn't stop you from choosing her.
And how rapidly Mary must have aged as she realised what was happening to her
       son, Jesus.

Never-ageing God,
when growing old in your service seems to be a very tiring process,
help us to remember the challenges you gave to these older people.

Teach us that we are never too old for new experiences.
Forgive us when we use our world-weariness to dampen the enthusiasm of youth.
Remind us that though we may be lacking in energy, they are not.
Keep us young in heart and spirit, even if our bodies protest,
for your world is a place of active love
and all of us can be involved in that,
whatever our age.

WHAT ARE WE DOING HERE?

Women's organisations in the church are constantly looking for other women to speak at their special events. Often this involves being given a complete order of service with set lessons and being asked to speak for ten to twelve minutes at the most. On one of these occasions the chosen Old Testament lesson was Exodus 17:1–7 and I began to wonder what it must have been like to be a woman in the crowd following Moses.

(This woman may well have been typical of the grumbling Hebrews who first moaned that they wanted to be free of slavery in Egypt – and then seemed to wish that they hadn't got what they'd asked for!)

CAN anybody tell me what we're doing here, all crowded round this big rock? Surely somebody should be out there looking for water. Why haven't they sent out a search party?

It's more than I can bear – I ask you – should anybody of my age be asked to stand around for hours in the sun like this, when we're all practically dying of thirst anyway?

We should at least be finding a nice cool cave where we could get some shelter till the evening – not standing around with another group of dim 'Moses followers' waiting for the next miracle.

I reckon Moses is overrated anyway. We weren't really *that* badly off in Egypt – why did *he* have to come back and stick his nose into *our* business? Admittedly we were slaves and the working conditions were hard – especially for the men with those slave-drivers on their backs all day – but we managed to eat and we had a roof over our heads and there was no big problem as long as we kept a low profile about our religion.

But that wasn't good enough for Moses, was it? I think he was just determined to make a name for himself. After all, the old ones said that he was once a part of the Egyptian court. And he still would have been, if he hadn't gone and killed one of the overseers, who was beating up one of our men.

Apparently Moses had one of those brainstorms, when he remembered his Hebrew roots, and he got really angry and then had to leave in a hurry and wasn't seen again for years. Until one day he just turned up at the court and demanded that Pharaoh let our people go free – because he claimed God had told him to do it!

He didn't get very far with Pharaoh, I can tell you that – and there weren't even many of our people on his side either in the beginning. A few hotheads maybe, out for revenge – and a few of the very religious that always had their heads in the clouds, expecting that God would send a deliverer. I ask you, would you have believed him at first?

But then things started to go wrong and people talked about these plagues as being a punishment from God on the Egyptians – Moses went on and on about it all the time. I didn't think there was much in it myself – just a series of coincidences really.

That was until we got that strange message about God threatening to kill the first-born child of every family, unless you were a Hebrew and painted blood on the lintel of your house.

I must admit that scared me a bit. You can't take chances with your children, can you? So we did the same as the others and it was really weird how our children were protected and the others weren't. You could hear the wailing of the Egyptian mothers all over the city.

Now that's when the real trouble started – because that's when we all had to get out of there in a real hurry. It was as well that we'd packed our bags and were ready to go. The Egyptians were far too busy with their mourning to notice us at first – and we got as far as the Red Sea before we heard them following.

Now *that* was another coincidence!

There were old tales of that sea sometimes drying up suddenly – something to do with winds and tides. I didn't understand it, but my husband had heard about it. And it just happened exactly at the time we got there! It was unbelievable!

Somebody at the front of the crowd said that Moses had stretched out his stick over the waters and they'd miraculously parted – but I ask you, how likely is that?

No, I think that we were lucky, just for once – but we had to hurry over because we knew it wouldn't last long.

And it didn't. Almost at the exact minute that our last old man stepped on dry land you could see the waters turning and coming back. Which was a bit of bad luck for the Egyptians who were halfway across in their chariots and couldn't get out of the way in time.

Serves them right, I say!

But that's why we're now in this hot thirsty crowd in the desert, waiting for another so-called miracle. We ran out of food very quickly – until we found out about this white stuff that appears on the ground overnight and is reasonably edible, although it doesn't keep and it hasn't really got a lot of taste. It'll get *very* boring, after a while.

But now we're out of water – and where has Moses come to look for it? In a rock! Honestly! I think he's a bit touched by the sun. You can't get blood out of a stone – and I'm sure he'll never find water in a rock.

Oh, hang on – there's a bit of excitement up at the front. I wonder what all the fuss is about?

What do you mean? He's struck water? Come on! You can't be serious?

He must have known there was a stream there already. But I'll bet he's saying that God told him.

I wish I had as much faith in God as he seems to have.

You *can* perform miracles with a faith like that!

JESUS LIVED A SIMPLE LIFESTYLE

When the Anglican Stewardship Association began to compile its anthology on giving, 'First Fruits', they asked for material from contributors to the 'Worship Live' periodical. The brief was specific; there seemed to be an abundance of writing about giving time and talents, but very little about giving money.
This hymn is a revised version of my original response to that challenge.

ALL FOR JESUS (8.7.8.7.)   *John Stainer (1840–1901)*

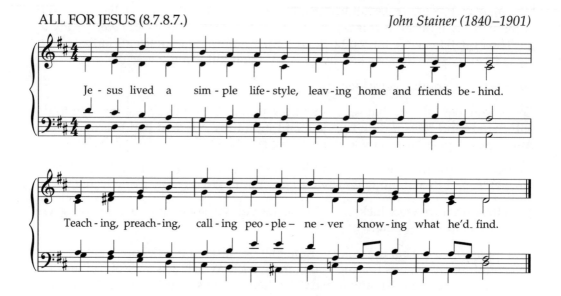

Jesus lived a simple lifestyle,
leaving home and friends behind.
Teaching, preaching, calling people –
never knowing what he'd find.

Reaching out to all and sundry –
beggar, blind man, leper, cheat.
Helping, healing, sharing, caring,
each one's need was his to meet.

On his feet were worn-out sandals.
On his back a dusty robe.
Little money, no possessions –
yet his message spanned the globe.

Now our world is far too selfish,
wealth and status are our creed.
Yet the poor are always with us,
begging that we meet their need.

Jesus, we would ask forgiveness,
we're so full of self-concern.
We should act with your compassion,
this world's values overturn.

Teach us, Lord, to set our standards
by your guidance, as we pray.
Help us follow your example,
living your concern each day.

WHO'S CALLING?

The people who responded to the personal call of Jesus in his day were a strange assortment of characters from all kinds of backgrounds.

What kind of people does he call today and has the world changed so much that our response would be very different?

JESUS called four fishermen.
He said, 'I'll make you fish for men!'
But that was back in history when
the fishing trade was strong.

Jesus called a taxman, too.
He said, 'I've work for you to do!'
But taxmen then were villains too –
not like they are today.

He called one man down from a tree.
He said, 'You come and follow me.'
But then it's plain for all to see
that life was simpler then.

He called all kinds of country folk.
He said, 'You come and bear my yoke.'
But farming words were what they spoke
back in those good old days.

He also spoke to learned men.
He said, 'You should be born again.'
But people's lives were different then,
when Jesus walked the earth.

If Jesus came to earth today,
who would he call to go his way?
And would he be prepared to pay?
Or who would follow?

For values are so different now,
no one would want to take a vow
to follow Jesus anyhow –
it's far too risky!

Yet still his voice calls clear and strong,
'Come follow me. You won't go wrong.
My love will last you all life long –
and that's a promise!'

WHY FISHERMEN?

The enemies of Jesus must have felt there was no real threat in the early days of his ministry. What danger could there be from a deluded carpenter whose chief followers seemed to be a group of fishermen? They wouldn't last long.

But Jesus chose well. Of course, they had their faults and their behaviour exasperated him at times, but they were tough and they had stamina. And one day it would become very clear why Jesus had chosen them.

One   Jesus called fishermen because they had the qualities he needed. They were simple and straightforward and said what they thought ...

Two   ... which gave them instant appeal to the ordinary people who crowded round Jesus.

One   They were used to rough living and being out in all weathers. They had a simple lifestyle ...

Two   ... which meant that they did not expect too much in the way of creature comforts and would be prepared to follow Jesus anywhere.

One   Their minds were uncomplicated. They were not tied up in ritual and rules like the stricter religious leaders. They were open to new thoughts ...

Two   ... even though it sometimes took them a long time to understand. But, once they understood what Jesus was saying, they did their best to follow it.

One   They were just the kind of people Jesus wanted for that time and that lifestyle.

Two   What kind of people does he want now?

One   He still wants ordinary people – like us!

Two   People who struggle through life sometimes and understand the problems other people face.

One   He wants people who care. About the world ...

Two   ... and about other people.

One   He wants those who can talk ...

Two   ... and those who can listen.

One	He wants young people with enthusiasm ...
Two	... and older people with experience and wisdom.
One	He wants people who are free to move around and follow his lead ...
Two	... and those who can stay and work in the area in which they live.
Together	We are just the kind of people Jesus wants for this time and this lifestyle.
One	But will we ask too many questions ... ?
Two	... or have too many reservations?
Together	Only you can answer that!

WE ARE KINGDOM PEOPLE

A friend rang late one night.

'We're doing our Christian Week at the guest house and we'll be studying the Beatitudes. We've been praying about it and I got a very clear message that God wants us to have a special hymn on the subject.'

'Err, ye-e-es!' I had a feeling that I knew what was coming next.

'The tune is the one set to "Onward Christian Soldiers" and the first line of the chorus is "We are kingdom people".'

'Err, ye-e-es!'

'You're the only hymn writer I know. Can you do it?'

'Well, I'm sure I can give it some thought.'

'We need it the day after tomorrow. Sooner would be good, then we can get copies made.'

At this point I muttered, under my breath, something distinctly un-Christian about God and my friend, but it didn't seem as if I had much choice in the matter.

'I'll see what I can do, but I can't promise.'

'Oh, I know I can rely on you,' she said and put the phone down with relief that she and God had sorted out the problem.

Did I? Well, the hymn was written on time and received enthusiastically, but I have smoothed off a few of the rough edges since then. But when God sets the challenge and timetable ...

WE ARE kingdom people
living every day
with the words of Jesus
teaching us his way.
We have many blessings
promised in God's word;
let us raise our voices,
make our message heard.
We are kingdom people,
blessed by God each day.
We will walk with Jesus
on our pilgrim way.

Bless the poor in spirit,
kingdom hopes are theirs.
Those who are in mourning;
God will dry their tears.
Meek ones will be given
all the earth to share.
Seekers after righteousness
find fulfilment there.
Chorus

To those who show mercy,
God will grant it, too.
And pure-hearted people
find that God is true.
Peacemakers find blessing –
children named by God.
Persecuted people
will have full reward.
Chorus

When we suffer evil
and false claims are made,
though they test and try us,
we are not afraid.
Prophets went before us
on this road to heaven;
we go on, rejoicing
in the promise given.
Chorus

ST GERTRUDE (6.5.6.5.D. and Chorus)

Arthur Sullivan (1842–1900)

We are king-dom peo - ple liv - ing ev - ery day with the words of

Je - sus teach-ing us his way. We have ma - ny bless - ings

prom-ised in God's word; let us raise our voi - ces,__ make our mes-sage

heard. *We are king - dom peo - ple,__ blessed by God each__*

day. *We__ will* *We will walk with Je - sus on our pil - grim way.*

LUKE'S BEATITUDES

The Beatitudes are a clear statement from Jesus about real values and the way in which his standards turn the world upside down. Taking them at face value they make no sense in the everyday world. So what do they mean?

How can being poor be a blessing?
Unless it means that you have no possessions to worry about,
or you're quite prepared to share the little you have,
or you know that you're at the bottom of the heap so you can't get any lower,
or it brings out the best in you,
or it means that people matter more than things?

Is that the kingdom of God?

How can hunger satisfy you?
Unless it means that if you have no food, then you're happy to eat anything,
or you get back to basics and eat more healthily when you do eat,
or you will never have the worry of obesity,
or you appreciate the true flavour of food when you have it,
or, if you get the chance, you have real pleasure in growing your own food,
or, failing everything else, you starve and don't have the misery of a long life?

Is that being satisfied?

How will weeping now make you laugh later?
Unless it means the tears will eventually wash away the sorrow,
or you will exhaust yourself with crying,
or friends will come along to cheer you up and support you,
or you'll make yourself look so horrible that you'll have to laugh at yourself in the
    mirror,
or your weeping may bring on a sympathy vote from others?

Is that laughing?

How will hatred from others bring a reward?
Unless it means that you know you must be getting through to them,
or they see that you have a different way of living,
or they are hostile to God,
or they can't live up to the standards you set,
or they don't want to listen, so they employ bully-boy tactics?

Is that rejoicing in heaven?

Who knows?
Jesus?
Or did he mean something else?

TRESPASSERS WILL ...

Our church planned a series of services based on the Lord's Prayer and the Minister and several Local Preachers got together to divide up and allocate the different themes. They gave me 'forgive us our trespasses' and reminded me that my Sunday was a Parade Service and the congregation would include lots of youngsters and several parents who only attended occasionally.

Some kind of dramatic performance seemed to be an essential element of this service.

(Two people come from opposite sides to meet in the middle – number two steps over an imaginary line.)

One   Hᴇʏ! Stop right there. This is my space.

Two   Eh! What do you mean? Where's your space?

One   Here. This side.

Two   This side of what? I can't see any lines.

One   There's a line right down the middle. This half is mine – that half is yours.

Two   What line? I can't see any line. There's no such thing as a line. (*Threateningly*) Show me.

One   (*Nervously*) Well, the actual line isn't actually there, you can't actually see it – but this half is actually mine and you shouldn't actually be in it.

Two   Oh, shouldn't I? Well, tell me why not. What'll you *actually* do if I don't move?

One   I'll ... I'll ... I'll ... prosecute.

Two   Prosecute! Prosecute! What on earth for?

One   Trespassing, that's what. You're on my side, so you're trespassing. Haven't you seen the signs TRESPASSERS WILL BE PROSECUTED?

Two   No. As a matter of fact, I haven't. First of all you've got imaginary lines, now you've got imaginary signs.

One   But you're still trespassing on my space.

Two   So what? Anyway I don't have to worry about what you'll do, 'cos God will forgive me.

One   What's God got to do with anything? It's my land you're trespassing on.

Two   Doesn't matter. It's God that'll forgive me – it says so in the Bible.

One   I don't believe it. Where does it say so in the Bible?

Two   It *actually* says it in the Lord's Prayer. It says, 'Forgive us our trespasses.' – See! All I have to do is to ask God and he'll forgive me – you've got nothing to do with it.

One   That can't be right. But, hey, wait a minute! I can check that. My Gran
             gave me this card thing with the Lord's Prayer on it. (*Finds scruffy card
             right at the bottom of a pocket and reads, then looks up triumphantly.*) Well,
             you're right, it's here – but it doesn't apply to you.

Two   What do you mean? Of course it applies to me. It applies to everybody.
             We all say it.

One   Yes, but there's a condition. You have to look at the next bit as well.

Two   What next bit?

One   This next bit here. It says, 'Forgive us our trespasses – as we forgive those
             who trespass against us.'

Two   So! What difference does that make?

One   Well, that means God won't forgive you, unless you forgive me.

Two   Forgive you for what?

One   Trespassing! (*Steps firmly over the imaginary line onto the other side. ACTION
             FREEZES*)

RICH FOOL

*There are many ways of bringing a parable up to date, but only one major reason for
doing so – to make it relevant to today's society.*
What might the rich fool be collecting today?

'Four Rolls Royces,
three Mercedes Benz,
two Lamborghini
safe within their pens.

The Rovers are all over.
Porsches are in the shed.
How I love to count my cars
while lying in my bed.

Bentleys are in the annexe
with a Jaguar or two,
but if they send that Cadillac,
then what am I to do?

I'll build a bigger garage.
Then the neighbours' eyes will pop ...'
But precisely at that moment
God said, 'Stop!'

JESUS, WHEN YOU LIVED ON EARTH

This prayer is stored on my computer under the title of 'designer jeans', because that phrase seems to say a lot about the values people place on fashion today.

Jeans are meant to be working trousers. They were originally designed as such and their natural companions are a checked shirt and a pair of workman's boots. That is how it should be.

But today there are jeans designed by fashion experts and sold at exorbitant prices. Most of them look the same anyway, apart from the all-important name on the label. Trainers are sold on the same principle and the advertising and fashion media puts tremendous pressure on people to buy the 'right' label. It takes a very brave parent to say 'no' and the credit card companies are only too happy to say 'yes' to people who continually increase their debts in order to fit in with fashion.

On to this scene strides Jesus, asking us to look at our values and the way we use our money.

And he sets us an example.

JESUS, when you lived on earth you didn't wear designer jeans, or labelled trainers, or carry luggage with the right name on it. You took the simple route, with practical clothes and no excess baggage.

Please help us to examine our values and priorities and to be aware of the message we give to others, if we insist on being as fashionable as they are.

Jesus, when you talked about money you praised those who gave sacrificially, challenged those who had too much money for their own good and urged people to be honest and to pay their due taxes.

Please forgive us those times when we are selfish in our use of money, believing that what we earn we are entitled to spend as we please. Keep us honest in our dealings and prompt us to generosity, as we respond to the needs of those who have nothing.

Jesus, you gave people your time and attention, dealing with each individual and their problems on a personal basis, even though you were aware of how much energy that drained from you.

Please strengthen us to face the demands that other people's needs place on our time and energy. Remind us that you never turn us away when we need you.

Jesus, your whole life was an example of giving to others.

Teach us how to be more like you.

RICH YOUNG RULER

The Minister and I were talking together after a service.

'Next week the subject is the rich young ruler,' he said, 'you know, I've always wondered what would have happened if he had said "yes" to Jesus.'

Two days later I contacted him again.

'I have a couple of scripts for you,' I said. 'Would you be interested in using them in your service?'

The next Sunday evening I sat in church and heard those same newly written scripts used as a two-point sermon by the Minister, Mark Haynes, who is a bit of an actor on the side.

It was the first time I had ever heard my own words preached to me as a sermon and it was an uncanny experience. The pieces could also be read by two voices as a dramatic performance.

Have you ever wondered what happened to some of the people Jesus dealt with? Did his teaching, healing, or advice have a long-lasting effect on their lives, or did some of them go back to their old ways? And what *did* happen to the rich young ruler? Perhaps he always wondered what a difference it would have made if he had done as Jesus asked – or maybe he changed his mind ...

The young man who didn't want to take advice

I MIGHT have known I wouldn't get the answer I wanted from that Jesus chap they'd all been talking about – although I did have real hopes that he would understand. Everyone kept telling me that he had an amazing gift for getting through to people. They said he talked to anybody – rich, poor, religious, or sinners. He seemed to deal with the ones that the rest of us have learned to ignore – beggars, blind people, prostitutes – even lepers and tax-collectors! I suppose that I thought my question would be an easy one, compared to their demands.

I have lived a good life and it's never been too much of a problem for me to do that. The odd mistake here and there, but my position in life has protected me from so many dangers and temptations. I suppose, just like everything else, I can afford to be good – and when you're giving all the orders and shouldering the responsibility it makes you look at life in a different way. You make your choice between honesty and crookedness very early in life – which is what I've done. Some of my friends have gone for the position of constant compromise, but then you're walking a tightrope all the time. I'd rather choose which side I'm on and stick with that.

But I do like to know where I will be at the end of it all. When you're rich you can buy your security. You know that anything you need, you can afford it. And being a figure of authority, you know your decisions will be respected. So, if you're a law-abiding citizen, like me, then your future must be secure.

But there always seems to be that one small niggling doubt ... so I decided to go to see Jesus.

When I asked about inheriting eternal life, I knew what it meant to inherit – I was already my father's heir. And there had never been a question about that inheritance, as long as I did nothing that would put me out of favour with my father. So what I wanted to check with Jesus was that I was doing the right thing in God's eyes, which would make me a part of his kingdom as well. And when he asked me whether I'd obeyed the commandments, I thought, 'That *is* all there is to it. I've no need to worry!'

Even when he said, 'There's just one more thing ...' I still had the time, in that instant before he said the next words, to think, 'Just one more – I'm sure I can cope with that!'

But then he said the last thing I expected him to say. 'Go and sell all you have.' Did he know how much that was? Did he realise it was a sacred inheritance from my father? What would I have left to live on?

And he wasn't finished. 'Give it to the poor.' What good would that do? I'd always given alms to the poor – that was part of my responsibility. But all the money I had and all the money my estate would produce! What would the poor do with all that? Of course, it might make them comfortable for a while, but they're not used to handling that amount of money. In no time at all they'd have squandered it on wine and women – or worse! – and what would my father have thought of that?

Then, on top of all that, Jesus had the nerve to say, 'Come and follow me.' Me! Join a bunch of fishermen with not two pennies to rub together! Wander round the countryside, not knowing where you would be from one day to the next, or the kind of people you would have to meet and deal with.

No – I couldn't do that!

If it had just been Jesus, then I might have considered it. He was a very charismatic man – there was no doubt about that. He attracted crowds wherever he went and some of the things he did were quite spectacular – healing lepers is something you don't see every day. He was a good teacher as well. Some of the things he is reported to have said were very profound and quite challenging. It would have been interesting to hear more.

So, if he'd allowed me to become one of his followers without the other conditions, I would have gone with great interest. I could even have smoothed the way for him – made sure he could afford comfortable accommodation and decent meals. Introduced him to a few influential people – I might even have been able to be a peacemaker when he got himself in trouble with the Pharisees and the teachers of the law. A discreet donation here and there could have covered a multitude of sharp words. Yes, in those circumstances, I could have done a lot for him. Money always talks.

But I don't think I would have been very good at being poor. Not for any length of time. I'm too used to my creature comforts. And to give up my position of responsibility to join such an odd group of people, following a man who was only a carpenter, when all's said and done ...

No! That was just too much to ask.

But I must admit I was sorry about it, all the same.

The young man who had second thoughts

I MIGHT have known I wouldn't get the answer I wanted from that Jesus chap they'd all been talking about, although I did have real hopes that he would understand.

And he did, of course – it was just that I didn't understand it at the time.

There I was, marching up to this carpenter with his band of – it must be said – rather odd-looking and scruffy followers. Me – with my stylish robes, my retinue of attendants and my total conviction that I was going to show Jesus that I was already well on the way to the kingdom of heaven – my wealth hadn't made me into a sinner! Looking back, it amazes me to think that I actually expected Jesus to be impressed. Rich, but modest; wealthy, but responsible and concerned about my standing in God's eyes. This was going to be one of those rare occasions when Jesus met a person of influence for whom he could have no criticism. I should have known better – but I didn't really know him then.

I started well, of course. I knew the commandments and I also knew I'd been behaving myself and had obeyed them – with the odd slip now and then, for which I had asked God's forgiveness and made the appropriate sacrifices.

But then, when I'd impressed him with my good behaviour, he suddenly looked me straight in the eyes and he seemed to be looking right inside me – right to the depths of my mind, my very being – and he was seeing the secret things that I didn't even know I was hiding from myself.

And he said those words that shook me to the core. 'One more thing – sell all you have and give it to the poor ...'

I don't remember hearing the rest, although I must have done because I remembered it later, but I was so devastated by the words 'sell' and 'give' that that's all I could think of at the time.

When I look back, I realise that some of the crowd must have had a good laugh at the expression on my face. I was just stunned and I remember turning away so disappointed and shocked that I can't remember the journey home. I presume my personal servants took care of me.

I didn't sleep properly for several weeks after that. 'Serves you right for trying to take advice from a carpenter!' I kept saying to myself. Looking back, I don't know how I kept going – habit, I suppose – because when I'd walked away from Jesus my first thought had been, 'Forget it!' but I knew I couldn't. When he'd looked into my eyes, he'd seen right through me and he knew what I needed.

I hadn't realised I'd become so used to my rich lifestyle that I depended on it for my satisfaction with life and God was taking second place. I was also used to my position of leadership and it had got to the point where I believed I had all the answers and was totally capable of controlling my life and the lives of others. I hadn't quite got to the point where I believed myself to be equal with God, but I was getting dangerously close to it.

This revelation finally came to me when I was pacing my bedroom at three-o-clock one morning. It hit me so hard that I had to sit down very suddenly on the bed with what is now the blindingly obvious thought – 'Jesus was right! You have led a decent life. You have done all that you should have done. But you're trapped. It's money you're depending on, not God – and Jesus could see that.' And at that point I also remembered what else he had said – 'When you've given it all up, come and follow me.'

I can't pretend it was easy. It wasn't! Selling my inheritance. Giving the money away, when all my instincts were to put some away for a rainy day. Just in case!

And then I had to *find* Jesus, before I could follow him. It wasn't too hard, because people were talking about him so much. But I'd taken so long in making my decision – and the settling of my affairs had been a very involved process, so by the time I caught up with Jesus they were already in Jerusalem and he was beginning to have so much trouble that I never got near enough to introduce myself to him and tell him that I'd finally done what he asked. I got the impression that he noticed me in the crowd one day and I seemed to sense a flicker of recognition – even a faint smile – but I'll never really know. They arrested him shortly after that and we all thought it was the end.

That really did make me ask myself whether I'd done the right thing, or whether I'd made a real fool of myself by taking the advice of a fanatic. But by then I had nothing to lose, so I hung around on the edge of things until the Feast of Pentecost.

Yes, I was actually in that crowd when Peter and the others came bursting out, full of the Spirit. They did seem drunk at first. But I was also one of the three thousand who became totally committed to the way of Christ that day. And that was when I discovered what real riches are.

Do I regret it?

Only that I didn't do it earlier – when Jesus first challenged me. It wasn't easy. Still isn't. But he knew what he was asking of me and I should have known that I could trust him. He was only asking me to get my priorities right, after all.

A RICH YOUNG MAN CAME SEEKING

This hymn was also written for the Anglican Stewardship Association's book 'First Fruits', although it has had a few minor alterations made to it since that was published.

Jesus did not say a great deal about money, but what he did say was very pointed. Some of those incidents are picked up in this hymn.

A RICH young man came seeking –
God's kingdom was his aim.
The law had been his guidebook.
His life was free from blame.
But Jesus asked the courage
to give his wealth away.
The young man turned in sorrow,
that price he could not pay.

The rich men's gifts were lavish
and made for public show.
The widow's gift was humble
and only God would know,
in giving to the Temple,
although her coins were small,
her gift had so much meaning
because she gave her all.

One boy brought loaves and fishes,
no other food was there,
but Jesus fed the thousands
and still had bread to spare.
The miracle of plenty
soon spread beyond that place.
That simple gift was offered,
then multiplied by grace.

Lord, keep our care for money
from turning into greed.
Help us to use it wisely
to meet each other's need.
For whether poor or wealthy,
we have so much to share
and open-hearted giving
will show your loving care.

ABEL (7.6.7.6.D.) *Reginald Barrett-Ayres (1920–81)*

A rich young man came seek-ing– God's king-dom was his aim. The law had been his guide-book. His life was free from blame. But Je-sus asked the cour-age to give his wealth a-way. The young man turned in sor-row, that

(last verse only)

price he could not pay.

WHEN A BLIND MAN CAME TO JESUS

As Jesus began to make an impression on people with his dynamic teaching and his healing ministry, it must have seemed that a whole new era was about to dawn. For some people that was a very personal experience as they were healed and given a new start in life. Jesus continues to lead from darkness to light and that is an eternal promise.

WHEN a blind man came to Jesus
asking for the gift of sight;
in those first few anxious moments
he could only see faint light.
Then the full truth dawned upon him,
broke through his eternal night.

When a widow, lost in grieving,
knowing that her son was dead,
followed, weeping, to his burial,
Jesus saw what lay ahead.
With compassion he approached her,
raised the boy up from his bed.

When the storm clouds of Good Friday
drained the light out from the sky,
broken ones who followed Jesus
could not see the reason why.
Only with the dawn of Easter
could their heads be lifted high.

When our lives are drowned in darkness,
when our faith is under strain,
we can also look to Jesus,
give to him our fear and pain.
Let his dawn light new horizons
as our hope is born again.

UGADALE (8.7.8.7.8.7.) *June Baker (1936–)*

When a blind man came to Je - sus

ask-ing for the gift of sight; in those first few anx-ious

mo - ments he could on - ly see faint light. Then the

full truth dawned up - on him, broke through his e - ter-nal night,

LAST TIME

broke through his e - ter - nal night.

WHEN PETER STEPPED OUT ON THE WATER

MY BONNIE LIES OVER THE OCEAN
(9.8.9.8. and Chorus)

Traditional Sea Shanty
arranged Christopher Maxim (1971–)

When Pe - ter stepped out on the wa - ter,_____ when Pe - ter stepped out on the sea,_____ his friends thought his ac - tion was sil - ly_____ and called out to him with this plea_____ 'Come back. Come back._____ Come back to safe - ty with us, please do. Come back. Come

back.   O   come back   to   safe - ty,   please   do.'

WHEN Peter stepped out on the water,
when Peter stepped out on the sea,
his friends thought his action was silly
and called out to him with this plea –
'Come back. Come back. Come back to safety with us, please do.
Come back. Come back. O come back to safety, please do.'

When Peter stepped out on the water,
when Peter stepped out on the sea,
so sure he could walk out to Jesus –
'It's OK. I'll do it. You'll see.'
'Come back. Come back. Come back to safety with us, please do.
Come back. Come back. O come back to safety, please do.'

When Peter stepped out on the water,
the waves underfoot made him think.
He felt the wind roaring around him
and slowly he started to sink.
'Come back. Come back. Come back to safety with us, please do.
Come back. Come back. O come back to safety, please do.'

When Jesus saw Peter was sinking,
he said to him, 'Peter, don't fret.
Take hold of my hand and I'll save you.
You've lots more to do for me yet.'
'Come here. Step out. Come face adventure with me,' he said.
'Come here. Step out. O come face adventure with me.'

Barring Jesus himself, Peter is my favourite New Testament person, without doubt.
He is brash, he is thoughtless, he speaks his own mind, he is boastful, he loves to
show off in front of others and he demonstrates his vulnerability by falling flat on
his face at times. He is a great comfort to all of us who admit to our own faults and
eccentricities. If Jesus could put up with Peter and still love him after the end, then
there is hope for us all.

This song is based on a typical incident in Peter's life. Although it was written
for children, all but the most solemn of adults sing it with great enthusiasm. Try it
with one side of the congregation singing the verses and the other responding with
the chorus, except for the last verse and chorus, which are sung together.

PETER

A story-poem written for performance to pre-teen groups, although it has been used frequently with older women's groups too. The strong rhyme and repetitive lines almost make it into a rap and it is best read aloud – even if your only audience is the empty room you're sitting in!

PETER the fisherman
walking by the lakeside
saw upon the pathway
a charismatic man.
Peter the fisherman
ran to the lakeside
said, 'Yes, I'll follow,
if you think I can.'

Peter the fisherman,
following his master
took on a swagger now,
thought he knew it all.
Peter the fisherman
said, 'I know you, Jesus!'
But Jesus shook his head,
said, 'You're in for a fall.'

Peter the fisherman,
always in the front line
speaking his mind in
his forthright way.
Peter the fisherman
put his big foot in it!
'Look,' said Jesus,
'go back and pray.'

Peter the fisherman
said, 'I'm on your side,
but don't go to Jerusalem –
it's not safe there!'
Peter the fisherman
was told by Jesus,
'Please don't tempt me,
I've a lot to bear.'

Peter the fisherman
said, 'I'll stand by you.
I'm not scared and
they won't shake me!'
Peter the fisherman
heard Jesus saying,
'You won't want to own me
 when I'm nailed to a tree.'

Peter the fisherman
didn't know what hit him –
Jesus arrested
and taken away.
Peter the fisherman
cowering in fear now,
accent betraying him,
couldn't even pray.

Peter the fisherman
ran from the cross
and hid himself away
in a secret den.
Peter the fisherman
couldn't quite believe it
when the women said,
'He's alive again!'

Peter the fisherman
said, 'It's all over.
Been a waste of time
and I'm going back to fish.'
Peter the fisherman
saw from his fishing boat
Jesus cooking supper
saying, 'Share my dish.'

Peter the fisherman
leapt towards Jesus.
'Do you really love me?'
he heard Christ ask.
Peter the fisherman
said, 'Lord, I love you
and I'll love your people, too.
If that's my task.'

Peter the fisherman
preached a great sermon.
Added three thousand
to the church one day.
Peter the fisherman –
what a transformation!
When the Holy Spirit
sent him on his way.

Peter the fisherman
preaching Christianity.
Wanted to keep it
for the Jews alone.
Peter the fisherman
up on the rooftop
heard God saying,
'It can't be done!'

Peter the fisherman
died upon a cross, too.
Though they say he did it
upside down.
But Peter the fisherman,
right to his dying day,
blessed that first morning
that Jesus came to town.

PETER – A NEW START

On the surface it appears that Peter never thinks very long about anything. He just speaks out and that's it. But he spoke out once too often on the night that he denied that he had ever known Jesus. How he must have tortured himself with those 'if only' words.

Here we look into the mind of Peter and imagine how he would have explained it afterwards. It was not his last chance, although it must have felt like it at the time.

Hello! My name is Peter – yes THAT Peter!

The one who said 'I will follow you anywhere, Jesus.' The one who was so full of himself when he recognised that Jesus was the Christ when nobody else seemed to. The one who was so proud when Jesus recognised him as a tower of strength and called him 'the Rock'. The one who set out to fight off the soldiers when Jesus was arrested. The one who denied even knowing Jesus when trapped by that young serving girl in the courtyard.

I'm that Peter. Not much to be proud of there, is there?

But I was different then.

I didn't have a bad start in life really. People think of fishermen as always being poor, but our family owned its own boats and you had to have a certain knowledge of business to succeed with so much competition around. And I was working with my brother, which made it a lot easier. Andrew and I are a bit like chalk and cheese, but that didn't do us any harm really. I was always prepared to take more of a risk – and he held me back if he thought I was doing anything really dangerous. We rubbed along together well enough and looked out for each other – and the great thing about Andrew is that he is very generous to those he cares about – and not just with money.

That was how I got to meet Jesus in the first place.

Andrew came rushing in all excited one day and told me that I must meet this very special teacher he had been talking to – and Andrew is not the kind of person who gets that excited unless there is something really special in the air. So, I went with him and, as you must know by now, that was the start of the biggest adventure of our whole lives. We were so thrilled by it all that we just left everything – family, friends, even the boats – and it's only afterwards that we realised how much of a shock that must have been for our father. But we weren't the only ones – and we did go back into the area occasionally – remember the time when Jesus healed my mother-in-law?

Life with Jesus was amazing! You never knew what would happen next. His teaching was different to the rest of them – and he really spoke as if he knew what he was talking about – not as if he'd just studied it to qualify as a teacher. The numbers of people who came to him for healing were overwhelming, yet he always dealt with as many of them as he could. He had a marvellous fund of stories – even if we didn't see the point of them all straightaway! And he certainly got the crowds on his side when he started on the Pharisees and Sadducees and the scribes – especially when he told them exactly what he thought of them – and even accused them of being hypocrites!

But that was also when the warning bells started ringing and we realised that he was putting himself in real danger, so we tried to *re-direct* him a little – not that he took any notice of us!

Yet we had some strange experiences with him too.

The strangest was at the top of that mountain – where we saw all that glowing light and those two men, who appeared to be Moses and Elijah. We hadn't a clue what to do, so I opened my big mouth again and suggested that we should build special places for them to stay – one of my dafter suggestions, I have to admit!

I don't think any of us understood what was going on with Jesus there, but we noticed that he started talking more about his death after that – almost as if that strange experience had been some kind of confirmation. I tried once to stop him talking about death and going to Jerusalem and he practically bit my head off and called me Satan, so I knew I'd put my foot in it again.

I kept doing that kind of thing, swearing allegiance one minute and letting him down the next, but the biggest mistake I made was the one I thought that I would never be able to put right.

We were all so tense in those last days with Jesus. I wouldn't say that we knew he was going to his death – we didn't – not really. He'd said he was, but we were so full of his ministry and the fact that the crowds always seemed to be on his side – and we just didn't see the danger signals.

And *none* of us could see what was happening inside Judas. Even to this day I can't understand his behaviour. He seemed to be as big a follower as any of us. But we were all different anyhow, so we didn't realise that he'd gone off on his own way and had been dealing with the enemy behind our backs.

But I have no right to be judgemental about him – not after what I did.

After all, I had been the one who protested when the soldiers came to arrest Jesus. I'd always been used to defending myself and I wasn't going to let them take Jesus if I could help it. It was the wrong thing to do, of course – or at least Jesus said it was – so I had to let him go without any more protest. But I was going to try to keep him in sight if I could. That was why I followed to the High Priest's courtyard and pushed my way to the fire – so that I could be near the action.

Unfortunately I didn't understand how the mood of the crowd was changing once Jesus was in enemy hands – and I just didn't think how dangerous it would be for me to be in that place. Andrew wasn't there to hold me back, I suppose.

It was only when that servant girl looked at me in that strange way and then asked me directly whether I was a friend of Jesus that I looked around and saw just how many hostile faces there were. So I panicked, didn't I? And I couldn't believe I was hearing myself denying that I knew Jesus. But once I'd said it I couldn't go back.

They seemed to ignore me for a bit after that, so I hung around, but then I must have said a few words to somebody about how cold it was and they recognised my northern accent and started on me again.

I was *really* frightened that time and my tongue got the better of me, as usual, and I found myself cursing and swearing that I didn't know this Jesus in any way.

Then I heard the cock crow – three times – and immediately I was back with the memory of Jesus telling me, only the night before, that I would deny him three times. I was devastated, because suddenly Jesus was looking at me and I knew that he knew what I'd done – even if he hadn't actually heard the words I'd said. I didn't know what to do with myself and I just wept and wept and then I ran away.

The next days are a blur. I knew they were crucifying Jesus, but I couldn't go anywhere near – I couldn't bear the sight.

But the most difficult thing to deal with was the fact that I'd betrayed him and I was never going to get the opportunity to say how sorry I was. What could I do to put it right? It was all over. Finished! Done! And I'd messed it all up – again!

They told me that Judas had committed suicide and I think I was the only one who felt any sympathy for him at that time. He'd been a betrayer, but then so had I. If I hadn't had family responsibilities to go back to I might have followed the same route myself. And when the women started talking about the fact that Jesus had come alive again I just didn't believe them – you don't get a second chance with life.

When they finally convinced me that it was true, it didn't make me feel any better – in fact I was terrified of facing him again, because he knew exactly what I'd done – even if I'd managed to hide it from the others. So I kept such a low profile that they wondered what was wrong with me. Which is why I escaped to the lakeside, the one place that I have always found I could get some peace.

Jesus knew where I was. Of course he did. And I didn't know where to put myself when he came towards me.

But then he asked me if I loved him! The answer was 'Yes', but how could he believe me after what I'd done? Three times I told him that I did – at first hesitantly, but then with more confidence – and then I suddenly realised what he was doing – he was forgiving me.

And he was giving me a new start – telling me to look after people for him. He knew I'd learnt my lesson the hardest possible way – *and* he knew I wanted a chance to start again.

You know the rest!

We didn't really take off in our work until the Holy Spirit came that Pentecost, but then things were never the same. All of us found hidden depths in ourselves and we were just as it had always been with Jesus – never knowing what was round the next corner, but always pushing on to new challenges and new opportunities.

A chance to start again after real failure – that's what Jesus gave me and that was the message I took with me wherever I went.

Jesus had always been in the business of changing lives and starting again – I should have realised that it applied to me as well!

THE SENTENCE

Here is another person given a second chance by Jesus. This woman was not innocent of the crime of which she was accused, but Jesus could clearly see the injustice of her being the only one condemned when the guilty man was considered to be blameless. She must have been terrified.

The piece was written for the 'Methodist Recorder' poetry competition in 2001. Although it was not a prizewinner, it was one of the twenty-seven chosen to be published in the competition results supplement.

My NAME – no matter – and my business, pleasure,
although the men had more of that than I.
The wicked one, the whore, the tramp, they called me.
and, deep inside, I knew it was no lie.

My life was sordid and so much in danger
from two-faced men who claimed the sin was mine –
and on that day a wife walked in and found us,
I was the only one accused of crime.

They dragged me out – the law said they could stone me –
along the streets, between the shouting men,
and at the front were Pharisees and lawyers –
I knew there was no point to protest then.

They took me up into the Temple courtyard –
why had they brought me to this holy place?
But suddenly the men were tense and silent,
their concentration fixed on one man's face.

I don't know how I knew that it was Jesus,
his path and mine had never crossed before.
I did know this would put me in more danger
for he had been in conflict with the law.

They wanted him to pass a judgement on me,
sure that he would not want to see me die.
But if he set me free they could accuse him
of claiming ancient law was just a lie.

He didn't even speak, or look up at them.
Some say he couldn't bear to see their hate.
But, when he asked the pure to start the stoning,
I thought, at last, that he had sealed my fate.

I heard the shuffling feet from all around me –
at any moment I would feel the pain,
but they were creeping out, their guilt inside them,
and I could feel a surge of hope again.

'Do none condemn you?' 'No,' I barely whispered.
'Then nor do I. Go then and sin no more.'
My life was spared; he'd given me my freedom.
Could I now change from what I'd been before?

It took some time to put my life in order.
I had to move away from spite and scorn.
But those few words from Jesus gave me courage
you'd almost think that I had been reborn.

COINCIDENTAL GOD

The phrase 'entertaining angels unawares' is one that has caught and held my imagination since the very first time I heard it read in church. In my life there have been many such people, although I doubt if any of them would have the remotest idea that they are considered to be heavenly visitors.

God of chance meetings and coincidental happenings,
help us to recognise where your hand has played its part.

We never know who we will meet,
or what is around the corner.
We cannot be sure which of our new encounters or experiences
will make a difference to our lives.

All we ask
is that you keep us alert to the possibilities
and aware of the opportunities
that you offer us.

We pray for the people we will meet today –
    for those we will greet with pleasure and recognition;
    for those we do not yet know, but may discover unexpectedly;
    for those who will challenge us, or teach us something new;
    for those who will need our help;
    and especially we pray for those we would rather not meet,
    that we may greet them with the same openness that Jesus used in his
        dealings with others.

Forgive us Father, those times when we fail to recognise the angels you have sent
    to us,
but please keep coming back,
so that one day we may become aware of the ways in which you are trying to
    reach us.

Help us to greet friend and stranger in your name.

COME SING A SONG OF FAITH

This hymn was written to the theme of faith, hope and love chosen by a church holding a creative arts weekend, the full story of which will be told later in the book. As this was an early effort at hymn writing to a subject it has been considerably altered since it first appeared.

COME sing a song of faith,
trust in God's constant word.
Born of the Spirit's breath,
in Jesus seen and heard.
Though testing times shake our belief,
faith whispers through our pain and grief.

Come sing a song of hope,
promise for future days.
Vision and strength to cope
in life's perplexing maze.
For though we live through troubled times,
the resurrection hope still shines.

Come sing a song of love
shown in a holy birth.
Loving so far above
all other love on earth.
A love that suffered pain and loss,
yet made a triumph of the cross.

Faith, hope and love hold fast.
Then, with God's final word,
faith realised at last.
Hope finds its longings heard.
And love will have so much to give
when with our God at last we live.

ATLANTIC BRIDGE (6.6.6.6.8 8.) *Valerie Ruddle (1932–)*

Come sing a song of— faith, trust in God's con - stant word. Born
of the Spi - rit's— breath, in Je - sus seen and heard. Though
test - ing times shake— our be - lief, faith whis - pers through our—
pain and grief.

LAST TIME

The Disciples' Way

Being a disciple is never easy.

It means accepting a constant learning curve and being humble enough to admit that the teacher knows best. After a certain length of time, which is determined by each individual, the temptation to believe that there is nothing more to learn is inevitable. We know it all. Just like the disciples of Jesus, who frequently displayed their faults and failings and even occasionally tried to tell Jesus where he was going wrong. Even after their lives were dramatically transformed by the power of the Holy Spirit at Pentecost, they still made mistakes and had difficulties with relationships and practical problems, just as we do.

Encouraging, isn't it?

This 'Disciples' Way' section reflects on the joys and problems of being Christians in an uncaring world and in churches that sometimes look as if they have lost their sense of direction and purpose.

It is not an easy route to take.

LIGHT FROM THE DARKNESS CAME

LITTLE CORNARD (6.6.6.6.8 8.)   *Martin Shaw (1875–1958)*

LIGHT from the darkness came
when first the world began.
Sun sent its glorious flame,
part of God's master plan.
So order out of chaos grew
and life was clean and pure and new.

God gave his people choice,
freedom of mind and will.
Heard their dissenting voice,
saw that they chose the ill.
He tried to bring the world from night,
but most loved darkness more than light.

God sent his light again,
prophet and priest and king.
Fired by his love they came
light for the world to bring.
But though they made his message clear
the people would not always hear.

God sent his only Son
living in light each day.
Knew that the light had won,
people could see his way.
Though crucified by cruel men
this light returned and rose again.

Followers of Jesus, all
now caught the Spirit's flame:
answered the Gospel's call,
spread light in Jesus' name.
And though the dark was always near,
the light of life would calm their fear.

We now that light receive,
pass on its shining ray.
Preaching what we believe,
living in love each day.
And so God's glory still is known,
that all may praise the love he's shown.

During the time that I attended Bishop Auckland Girls' Grammar School, a school song was written – though not by me. As I remember it, the second and final verse ran –

'In that town now stands a school
built where once the rushes blew.
Built to be a seat of learning
and those pioneers knew
that we, too, the torch would carry
through the years with love and pride.
Stands the school! The torch still burns.
We guard the flame and pass it on.
Auckland stands! The torch still burns.
We guard the flame and pass it on.'

Typical of its time – or even of before its time – that stirring schoolgirl sentiment had long been forgotten. But the words must have been lurking somewhere in my subconscious mind, as I can see clear echoes of them in the phrases of this hymn. It was written on a train, travelling to a creative arts weekend with the theme of 'light', and the words are set to one of my favourite tunes, LITTLE CORNARD. It is the first of my hymns that I felt had any kind of merit and I look at it now with equal measures of affection and criticism.

It seems right that it should take its place at the beginning of this 'Disciples' Way' section, because it was the start of my serious journey into writing hymns. God's call can lead us in all sorts of directions, but I do firmly believe that one of our primary tasks as Christians is to bring God's light into the world of the everyday – whatever century we may live in.

HEARING THE CALL

Christian discipleship begins when we hear a call from Jesus to change direction and follow him. Sometimes this comes as a total surprise as our lives seem to be heading in the direction we have set for ourselves, but Jesus calls us to think again and consider other options.

We tend to forget what an upheaval it was for those first disciples of Jesus. Their lives were settled and ordered, with just a hint of restlessness here and there. But Jesus said, 'Come!' and they did. Have we the courage to do the same?

It's NOT always easy to hear your call, Jesus.
Our lives are so busy and our everyday business doesn't give us much time
    for the unexpected meeting.
But on that shore you called those men away from the everyday.
They had been fishing – as usual – and didn't ever expect to be doing anything else.

We have our routines and our expectations too and our vision can be very narrow
    at times.
Help us to be aware of the times when you are trying to get a word in edgeways.
And, if we manage to hear you, grant us the courage to respond as the fishermen did.
They were glad to be adventurous.
Remind us, Jesus, that we should be the same.

COMPELLING GOD

The call to discipleship is not the same for everyone. For some the direction is clear and compelling; others only know they want to follow Jesus but feel that they have no particular talent to offer. There is the danger that this can lead to some Christians feeling inferior in their calling, while others are so convinced of their direction that unintentionally they create an air of superiority around themselves.

We are reminded of this danger in Paul's Letter to the Roman church. We are also reminded that there are many different parts to the one body of the church, but we all need each other if the body is to function properly.

COMPELLING God,
there is an urgency about your love and your call
that insists that we respond to it.
There is so much work to be done
and we need your guidance to show us the right way to do it.

But although our eyes are fixed on you,
keep us aware that we are part of the whole body of the church
and that feet, hands, heart, ears, voice
and every other part of us
is dedicated to you.

Save us from being too self-absorbed.

GOD OF THE UNEXPECTED

The original building of the Methodist church at Bolton Junction in Bradford, West Yorkshire was set on a main road site not far from a major crossroads. It was a prominent, but plain, rectangular building with a high-ceilinged chapel and a hall underneath, a large vestry and a couple of side rooms. The chapel gallery had been partitioned off to provide extra meeting space and there was a downstairs kitchen next to the hall – the hall having inconvenient pillars in the middle, holding up the chapel. It was not an easy building to work in.

In the 1980s major structural problems began to appear and it was evident that serious decisions would have to be taken about the future of the church on that site.

There were about sixty members, a high proportion of them being around and over the age of sixty. Many discussions took place. Should they merge with another church? Should they sell the site and all move somewhere else? Should they spend a great deal of money on repairs? Or, the most daring suggestion of all, should they pull down the old building and put a new, more suitable, suite of premises in its place?

After a great deal of heart-searching and prayer the members decided to take the last option because they believed that was what God wanted them to do. They set a certain fund-raising target and believed that if they could reach that by the following Easter, then God was confirming their decision.

Many of the congregation were at that stage in life where they could have sat back and said, 'Not at my age!' but they didn't do that. They took on this unexpected challenge with drive and enthusiasm and conviction. This is the second of the two 'theme' songs written to support and encourage their efforts. The tune to this piece with the chorus is also by Graham Wilkinson, but it can be sung without the chorus to any suitable 7.6.7.6.D. tune.

God of the unexpected,
you take us by surprise.
For though we're full of knowledge
and feel so worldly-wise,
we sometimes miss your pattern –
we're so set in our ways –
we need your clear directions
to guide us through the maze.
Direct us, Lord, and help us
to see our way ahead,
that other generations
may trace your pattern's thread.

Sometimes when you are calling
we cannot hear your voice,
for some work that you give us
we would not do by choice.
Yet when we take your challenge
and cautiously move out,
we find you there before us
to help us through the doubt.
Chorus

Lord, lead us to the future,
whatever it may be.
We will trust you completely,
for only you can see.
Lord, you have led so many
who put their trust in you,
teach us by their example
to welcome what is new.
Chorus

God of the unexpected,
you break into our time
to help us take our places
in faith's unending line.
We're part of your great pattern
of witness, love and praise.
Renew us, Lord, and fit us
to serve these coming days.
Chorus

UNEXPECTED (7.6.7.6.D. and Chorus)   *Graham Wilkinson (1958–)*

God of the un - ex - pect - ed, you take us by sur - prise. For though we're full of know - ledge and feel so world - ly - wise, we some - times miss your pat - tern – we're so set in our ways – we need your clear di - rec - tions to guide us through the maze. Di - rect us, Lord, and help us to see our way a - head, that o - ther ge - ne - ra - tions may trace your pat - tern's thread.

© Copyright 1997 Stainer & Bell Ltd

DREAMS AND VISIONS

In churches everywhere there are many restless young people who are frustrated by what they consider to be very old-fashioned ways in church worship, mission and organisation. They long to change things and to do it as quickly as possible.

On the other hand, some elderly people who make up the majority of many congregations are genuinely disturbed by the idea of change and fear that it would sweep away everything that is familiar to them.

This 'Dreams and Visions' piece grew out of a conversation overheard at the breakfast table in a Christian hotel, where four elderly people were discussing how much they hated change in the church and blaming young people for it. At the time I was very involved with the members of a young people's group who were showing an equal frustration with the older people who seemed to be holding them back.

The next day I had been asked to take morning prayers in the hotel and found the passage from Joel (quoted at the end of this piece) was irresistible. It gave me the opportunity to talk about the dedication of these young people and to assure the older ones that the faith of both groups was based on the same call of Jesus and dedication to him. The rest was a matter of style.

It could have gone very wrong indeed, but obviously God's hand was in that morning worship and one of those same elderly ladies shook my hand and admitted that she would have to think again. All four of them left with a new determination not to be so critical, but to try to encourage the young Christians that they knew.

We are all disciples, whatever our age.

ONE is an older person, TWO is young, and READER can be any age.

One   I DREAM about the times that used to be – when the churches were full, when we had special services and events and everybody came. Those were the days when all our spare time was taken up with church and Sunday School and events like concerts and pantomimes and socials, Bible studies and fellowship meetings. Life was good then. All my dreams are golden. There were some bad times, but we got through them and those memories fade. What I remember most is singing the old hymns with a choir leading and the music being overwhelming – and the great preachers thundering out their message and keeping us in our seats for hours. If only today's youngsters could understand how much it filled our days and gave us a reason for living. There was so much that was good about it. Wouldn't it be wonderful if the churches were filled again today?

Two   I have this vision of all kinds of people being brought to Jesus and then gathering together in a great crowd to worship him. I can see it all now. Young and old, children and parents, all coming to find out about our wonderful God. I haven't been a Christian very long, but it's had an amazing effect on my life and I can't wait to share it with others. I read the Bible all the time. I've just discovered this new translation which really speaks to me. And some of the songs I've learnt since I got to know God have really touched the centre of my being and I want to share them with other people. I want to tell people of my own generation what a difference it makes to be a Christian. I want to work to change the world – to make it into God's world, with his justice and peace and everyone living in harmony and no more poverty and exploitation. Wouldn't that be wonderful? But I don't think the older people like the idea of my having so much energy. They probably think I'll grow out of it!

One   I dream of the past, because I have more of the past than the future. The young don't understand.

Two   I have a vision of the future because it stretches so far ahead of me. The old can't see that.

One   I dream of the past because it is the root of my faith which has seen me through life. Change disturbs me.

Two   I have a vision of the future when I can do great things for God. Change excites me.

One   I can reflect on my life and faith experiences and share those lessons with others. That's what life has taught me.

Two   I want to get up and go and take action and make an impact. I'll learn as I go along.

One   I have a dream that is centred on God.

Two   I have a vision that is given by God.

One   A dream centred on God.

Two   A vision given by God.

One   On God.

Two   By God.

Reader   God says, through the prophet Joel –
'Afterwards I will pour out my Spirit on everyone:
your sons and daughters will proclaim my message;
your old people will have dreams, and your young people will see visions.'

Joel 2:28

And through Paul, God says –
'There are different kinds of spiritual gifts, but the same Spirit gives them. There are different ways of serving, but the same Lord is served. There are different abilities to perform service, but the same God gives ability to all for their particular service. The Spirit's presence is shown in some way in each person for the good of all.'

1 Corinthians 12:4–7

CAPTIVATING GOD

This prayer follows the idea of 'Dreams and Visions' and encourages cooperation between all age groups.

CAPTIVATING God,
you have imaginative ways of connecting with people
and can challenge young and old and everyone in between.
Is it because every generation is the same to you?
You have no grandchildren – only children.

This is not always easy for us to understand.

Teach us your way of being family, with all of us as brothers and sisters.
Then age will not build barriers as we adventure together with you.

LORD, YOU CALL US

ANGEL VOICES (8.5.8.5.8 4.3.)   E. G. Monk (1819–1900)

Lord, you call us to your ser-vice, each in our own way.

Some to car-ing, lov-ing, heal-ing; some to preach, or pray;

some to work with qui-et learn-ing, truth dis-cern-ing, day by day.

LORD, you call us to your service,
each in our own way.
Some to caring, loving, healing;
some to preach, or pray;
some to work with quiet learning,
truth discerning,
day by day.

Life for us is always changing
in the work we share.
Christian love adds new dimensions
to the way we care.
For we know that you could lead us,
as you need us,
anywhere.

Seeing life from your perspective
makes your challenge plain,
as your heart is grieving over
those who live in pain.
Teach us how, by our compassion,
we may fashion
hope again.

Lord, we set our human limits
on the work we do.
Send us your directing Spirit,
pour your power through,
that we may be free in living
and in giving
all for you.

Occasionally a piece of writing is started and then seems to grind to a halt. Somehow the idea will not develop, or the rhyme scheme or metre proves more difficult than anticipated and the words will not flow on to the paper.

This hymn had two false starts and a change of tune before the words began to come together. It needed the impetus of an approaching competition entry date to make me work hard to pull it into shape. It was one of my two entries for the Methodist Local Preachers Mutual Aid Association's competition to celebrate their 150th anniversary and was published by them in the resultant book, 'Faith for the Future'.

The hymn celebrates the different ways in which we are called by Jesus and reflects on how our perspectives change as we take the path of discipleship. It was written to the tune ANGEL VOICES.

RECOGNITION

*Look back at your life and try to count how many people have been God for you over
the years. Some of them, probably most of them, would never believe it and often it
is only when you look back that you can see it clearly for yourself.*

*My disciple's journey has been peopled with an amazing variety of characters.
Allow me to introduce you to some of them.*

WHEN I was a child
God wore a flowered overall,
kept a best coat in mothballs
with a hat for church on Sundays,
was slightly eccentric
and a substitute Granny.

I didn't recognise her.

When I was thirteen
God wore the sober suit
of a teacher-preacher.
He lived in a tin chapel
with a pot-bellied stove
and cared about teenagers.

I introduced myself to him.

When I was sixteen
God wore a dog-collar
and carried a well-thumbed Bible.
He held a mirror
into which I looked
and saw myself
as he saw me.

I cried and talked to him properly for the first time.

As I grew older
God wore countless pairs of jeans,
baggy jumpers, T-shirts and sweatshirts,
trainers, boots and sandals.

Once he had a Beatle haircut.
Moved on through beards, flowers and Afghan coats,
skirt lengths from mini to maxi,
red braces, baseball caps,
high heels, low heels,
working and wellington boots.

He wore corduroy, velvet, manmade and natural fibres,
anoraks, duffel coats, overcoats, jackets,
waterproofs, sheepskin and leathers,
overalls, white collars, blue collars,
uniforms of all shapes and sizes and both sexes
and a rainbow array of ecclesiastical robes.

I never knew where he would turn up next,
but it was good to meet with him so often.

When I am old
will he have the long beard and white hair
of the artist's portraits?
Or will she wear a starched apron,
or yet another overall
and smile as she hands me a cup of weak tea?

Will I recognise her?

No matter.
He knows me.

ENCOURAGING GOD

*How many of those people who encouraged us along the way ever knew how much
we appreciated them? It is so easy to take people for granted and we know how
disappointed and disillusioned we sometimes feel when it happens to us.*

*One of our major tasks in the church should be to build each other up. This piece
was written for a local prayer diary, which was intended to build up concern and
fellowship between different churches in the area.*

ENCOURAGING God, we all need a little praise now and then to give a lift to our spirits.
We need to feel needed and appreciated
and far too many people seem to want to criticise and condemn.
Would it be too much to ask for a little boost to the confidence today?

But if we are feeling like that,
then so are many others and what are we doing about it?

As you encourage us,
help us to watch our own words with other people,
so that we give to others the support which we hope to receive from them,
for we are all part of your living, growing family.

PRAISE OUR GOD'S CREATIVE WORD

BUCKLEY-SAXON (7 7.7 7.)   *Paul Bateman (1954–)*

Praise our God's cre - a - tive word by which life on earth__ was stirred. When he spoke all worlds_ be - gan, from the cha - os came a plan.

PRAISE our God's creative word
by which life on earth was stirred.
When he spoke all worlds began,
from the chaos came a plan.

Praise for those who left their all
in obedience to his call.
Pilgrim, prophet, priest and king,
God's clear word they sought to bring.

Praise to Christ who came to earth,
prophecy fulfilled in birth.
Faithful people saw God's plan,
word translated into man.

Praise for all who heard Christ's voice,
made his way of life their choice.
Saw his cross up on the hill
God's redeeming work fulfil.

Praise God for the Easter dawn
with the word of life reborn
and for Pentecostal grace,
setting Christian hearts ablaze.

Praise the Spirit who inspires,
lights in us those holy fires;
drives us on to preach God's word
by which lives of faith are stirred.

When I first responded to the call of Jesus I had no idea where it would lead me, but it soon became evident that I was being called to preach. Within the Methodist system there were no barriers to a teenage girl responding to that call and I became fully qualified as a Methodist Local Preacher within days of my twentieth birthday.

Since then, my priority as a Christian has been to reach out to people with the word that is appropriate to them. For me, writing is an extension of that call.

This hymn explores the idea of God's spoken word in the beginning and the preached word, which has continued to relate God to his people.

CREATIVE GOD

Although the basis of the Christian message has remained the same, the way in which it is presented has to be constantly refreshed by each new generation of preachers. It is not easy to do this and all preachers need our prayerful support.

CREATIVE God,
your amazingly varied world is a constant source of wonder
and we are most startled
by the fact that you put the same creativity into each one of us.

Some of us use that gift in very practical ways,
others are gifted with imagination and insight.

Bless all those who lead worship
and inspire them with your inventiveness
to re-interpret your eternal message
with freshness and clarity.

A BROKEN BODY

The early disciples of Jesus saw many miracles and heard inspirational teaching directly from the lips of the Master. Yet they still had questions and doubts and did not understand everything.

We often wish we could have been there and are certain that we would have understood more than they did.

Our faith comes in 'crumbs from the Master's table' and pieces torn from any loaf are always ragged and uneven in size. So sometimes faith leaps ahead, sometimes there is barely enough to hold on. Yet, as crumbs are torn from a common loaf, so all our insights and glimpses of God come from a common source and, whether they are great or small, they are all steps along the way.

This piece was written for the 'Methodist Recorder' poetry competition in 2000 and although it was not a winner, it was published in the poetry supplement of the best entries.

FRAGMENTED is our picture of God:
fractured glory like stained glass.
Christ in everyday eyes,
Spirit whispers of inspiration,
creation unwrapping Creator.

Fragments are food for our souls:
splintered shards of conviction,
half-heard echoes of challenge,
breath-catching insights in worship,
petitions fulfilled by coincidence.

Fragments are our offering to others:
tokens of love to emptiness,
a sympathetic touch for tears,
coins or cheques for poverty,
gospel words here and there.

Fragments are all we take from the table:
crumbs from a common loaf,
sipped wine from a cup,
forgiveness and blessing
in the measure we set for ourselves.

Yet, fed by scraps of faith
torn from Christ's tortured body,
we see resurrection power:
transformation into wholeness
offered through fragmented people.

OPINIONS

Worship should really be the central part of the activity of each church, but it can lead to division and dispute in congregations. Some churches try to resolve the problem of changes in worship patterns by having a separate service, which can be used to experiment with new materials and formats. It does not always solve the problem and does pose the question of whether some people are worshipping in the right spirit.

This piece has some local and specific references, but can be adapted to suit most churches or situations by the simple substitution of a few words.

(Two old gossips – male or female. Adapt where necessary.)

One   'ERE! What do you reckon to this midweek 'Praise and Worship' thing then?

Two   What's that?

One   You know! It's on the notice sheet every month. They even put it in the Church magazine sometimes.

Two   Oh! Well, that's why I couldn't think what you meant. I don't read that Church magazine much.

One   No. Apart from making sure I'm not dead and checking up on who's ill, I don't read it much either.

Two   I mean, who needs a Minister's letter every month?

One   Precisely! But he does tell a good story, doesn't he?

Two   Specially when there's kids in church.

One   Mm! I do wish he wouldn't shout so much though. He nearly deafens me, what with my hearing aid and everything.

Pause

Two   What was it you asked me earlier on?

One   I can't remember ... oh yes, about this 'Praise and Worship' thing.

Two   Well?

One   Well, what do you think about it?

Two   I don't think about it very much, to tell you the truth.

One   Neither do I, really. But apparently they're keen to get more people involved in it.

Two   I'm not surprised. Do you know anybody who goes? I don't.

One   Well, there's one or two of those noisy types go – you know, the ones who sometimes clap in church when we sing that 'Give me oil in my lamp' thing.

Two   Yes! Well that's what 'praise and worship' means, doesn't it? Happy, clappy and putting your hands up in the air.

One   You wouldn't catch me doing a thing like that.

Two   Nor me. It's not reverent.

One   I mean, you're not meant to be grinning all over your face in church, are you?

Two   Except when the Minister tells his stories, of course. He even makes me laugh sometimes – but I try not to make it too loud.

Pause

One   You know, I think they must be giving up on this midweek worship. That's why they'll be asking people about it.

Two   Well, I can't see the point of it anyway. Surely you get enough services on a Sunday, without having them during the week as well.

One   They're supposed to be different to the Sunday ones.

Two   But why do you need anything different? I like what I'm used to.

One   Somebody told me they have drama in them nearly every time.

Two   Oh, I don't like that! People bobbing up and down, trying to act. They should leave that to the professionals.

One   And they don't use the hymn book very often either.

Two   There! I told you! Happy clappy!

One   They use that overhead projector thing – supposedly so they can do all sorts of new stuff.

Two   Well, there you go then! Always wanting to change! I prefer the old Methodist Hymn Book myself. I can't be doing with all this new music and words.

One   Apparently they get speakers from all kinds of different places. They've even had Anglican vicars there – and Americans! *And the Superintendent Minister!*

Two	Oh well, that says it all.
One	And they let them just sort of stand up and talk – not like a proper sermon.
Two	Hmph! They'll be letting the congregations ask questions next.
One	And do you know, they actually use the big chapel for this service?
Two	But I thought there weren't many people went to it?
One	There aren't. But apparently it has to be thought of as a mainstream church activity.
Two	They should put them in a back room – where they belong. It's only a minority, after all. And putting them in there would make sure it stayed that way.
One	Don't get so het up about it!
Two	Well, they annoy me sometimes. They're all 'holier-than-thou' types, when all's said and done.
One	But the Minister goes as well. Apparently he never misses it, unless he's got a previous engagement.
Two	But does he really want to *be* there?
One	He *says* he enjoys it.
Two	Well, he would, wouldn't he? Another thing for him to take charge of.
One	They say he takes a back seat a lot of the time.
Two	So, that's another reason not to go then. Don't these people know anything about having a trained person in charge of things?
One	Apparently not.
Two	Anyway ... why are we talking about this?
One	I don't know, really. Something to fill the time, I suppose. I just saw the notice about it on Sunday – and wondered.
Two	Well, I've got better things than that to do on a Thursday night. It's usually a good night on the telly.
One	But you never know about anything until you've tried it, do you?
Two	That's what they said about the Titanic!

GOD OF PAST GENERATIONS

It is fairly obvious from the pattern of this hymn that it was written to celebrate an anniversary. The hymn won fourth place in the 150th anniversary competition for the Methodist Local Preachers Mutual Aid Association and appeared in their book 'Faith for the Future'.

It is always good to recognise our heritage and be thankful for it, but we live in today's world and must cope with the situations we meet here. Then we can safely leave the future in God's hands, as long as we remember that we have our part to play in shaping it for the next generation.

GOD of past generations,
we offer thankful praise
for those of faith before us,
their wisdom and their ways.
So clearly in their living
your guiding hand appears
to keep their loving witness
alive throughout the years.

God of the present moment,
we live with you today;
though rush, routine and crisis
may often block your way.
Help us through work and worship
to keep ourselves aware
of how you call us, daily,
to show your love and care.

God of the unknown future,
wherever you may lead,
keep us alert and open
to meet each moment's need.
And in those times of trouble,
so hard to understand,
our fears, our hopes, our longings,
we place within your hand.

BRAMHALL (7.6.7.6.D.)   *Ian Sharp (1943–)*

God of past ge-ne-ra - tions, we of-fer thank-ful__ praise for
those of faith be - fore us, their wis-dom and their_ ways. So
clear - ly in their liv-ing your guid - ing hand_ ap - pears to
keep their lov-ing wit - ness a - live through-out the_ years.

Descant for verse 3

SACRIFICE

Many years ago I wrote a meditation for Good Friday, which detailed the brutality suffered by Jesus during his trial and execution. A few days later I overheard someone grumbling about the constant demands on her purse from special appeal envelopes. The contrast between the two attitudes to sacrifice was so outstanding that I found it hard to believe that she had been present when the meditation was used. This poem arose from that situation.

THE MILDEST suffering was the mockery
by raucous Romans with their royal robes
and cruel crown of thorns
pressed into the skull.
He did that for me.

Then there was the whip
with knotted nuggets of metal meshed into the thongs
tearing the tender flesh
when hurled by a heavy hand.
He did that for me.

And the nails
piercing, pointing, penetrating
and hammered down hard to make sure they held.
He did that for me.

And the cross
and the hanging from his hands
and the scorching sun
adding the final insult to his injury.
It doesn't bear thinking about!
I seldom do!

What do I do for him?
Suffer a twinge of conscience
as I cast my reluctant coins on the collection plate
and sit in solemn silence in a Sunday Service.

THE USE OF MONEY

If we are serious about our commitment to Christ then it affects our whole lifestyle. Money is an important part of all our lives. How do we reconcile our everyday financial demands – and the luxuries we indulge in – with our call to help others? We feel guilty if our lives are too comfortable. We need guidance to get the balance right.

WE FEEL guilty Lord, because we have been given so much while others have
so little.

Help us to recognise our responsibilities, Lord –
    to give our money in ways which will help the most,
    sometimes in regular giving to a known cause,
    sometimes spontaneously, as the need arises.

    to spend our money fairly,
    remembering that what we pay is meant to help others to a reasonable
        standard of living.

    to invest our money ethically,
    so that in sensible provision for our own future we are also supporting those
        industries and commercial enterprises that treat their workers justly, or
        those mutual groups which offer beneficial support to each other.

    to use our money wisely for the well-being of family, friends and community
    and in support of those initiatives which will help to shape your world more
        effectively into your pattern.

Forgive our occasional extravagances Lord, for you are a loving and understanding God, but teach us how your extravagance works in your total and outrageous generosity to your children. Help us to learn from you, Lord, that sacrificial giving is also demanded of us and our guilty feelings about the poverty of others are one of the ways in which you urge us to take action.

Lead us Lord, into an understanding of your will in the right use of our money – for your world's sake. Amen

SHARING GOD

One of the challenges we have to face when we follow Jesus is to ask ourselves what financial demands will result from this commitment. Other pieces on this theme are scattered throughout this book. This prayer acknowledges that giving in some ways can be fun, but it is not always so.

    Sharing God,
    you have ways of opening our eyes to the needs of others.
    This encourages us to use energy, effort and skills
    to help our favourite good causes and,
    although it is hard work,
    we often enjoy it and feel that it is worthwhile.

    But your sharing goes deeper than selling a flag,
    or doing a sponsored walk,
    even if those things are not easy.

    Encourage us
    when sharing your love is the last thing we really want to do.
    Teach us that those are the times when you need us most.

REVELATION

For many Christians discipleship means service in a specific church building. This can take many forms: leading worship, working in the kitchen, being on a committee, arranging flowers, playing music or singing, or one of the many other jobs that are necessary to keep the church running smoothly.

The more practical tasks can become so mundane that they lose the sense of service to God unless he prompts us to be aware of his presence. This can happen at the most unexpected times.

CLEANING rota again.
I enter church,
duster and polish
ready for action,
to find that, once again,
I am the first.

Standing alone,
the silence is alive.
Creeping around
come memories of prayer –
the walls releasing energy –
devotion of countless Christian
seekers for truth.

Overwhelmed,
I sit to take it in.
But Nonconformity
is not enough
and, slightly foolish,
I feel bound to kneel
before those silent witnesses.

How many prayers
of thankfulness and hope –
and countless tears –
have been heard here?
Vows have been made
and many partings known.

How many children,
fidgety and bored,
have first glimpsed truth
unknowingly?
And have the lonely,
lost and frightened,
bewildered or bereaved,
found comfort?

Do people feel inspired
by this place
which simply speaks to me
of old familiarity?

Cloaked in quiet contemplation,
answers enveloped me –
and God whispered,
'You, too.'

Though seeming more,
it was but minutes,
then traffic noise broke through
and voices,
as the other folk
arrived to help.

Hastily,
I grabbed polish,
pretending industrious inspection
of a chair leg –
to explain my kneeling.

The church and I
have never felt
the same about each other
since that day.

THAT BLOOMING FESTIVAL

*Flowers in church display both the creative power of God and the creative skills of
the flower arranger. Occasionally this is taken one step further and a complete Flower
Festival is arranged when many people can demonstrate their creativity with flowers.
These occasions are greeted with great pleasure by almost everyone. But there may
be some exceptions ...*

THERE were flowers in the entrance hall
and flowers on the stairs.
There were flowers on each pew end
marching up the aisle in pairs.
There were flowers in the pulpit,
theme of 'Christ the Living Word'
and so many round the organ pipes
no music could be heard.
Each window was a parable
interpreted in green.

The communion rail was garlanded,
the font could not be seen.
The cross was red carnations,
bread and wine placed at its feet
and the roses and the asters
beckoned us to 'Take and eat.'
'The Storm Was Stilled' with larkspur
and delphiniums, deep blue,
and sunshine yellow blooms proclaimed,
'Remember God Loves You.'

So many people came to look –
they were not asked a fee –
until, of course, they went downstairs
to have cream scones and tea.

But the Flower Festival at church
was hailed a great success –
unless you were on the cleaning team
that faced the final mess!

SOUNDS

*All women preachers are constantly asked to speak at women's groups and many of
these are still called 'Ladies' Meetings'.*

*Often they are held in a room deep inside the building and are very difficult to
find on a first visit. Except for one thing. All you really have to do on entering the
church is to stand and listen. Some meetings announce their presence at the other
end of the street!*

CHAIR-LEGS scrabbling,
voices babbling,
teacups clattering,
noisy chattering,
money chinking,
piano tinkling,
laughter sounding,
echo rebounding,
noise is rising,
not surprising!
Someone's yawning.
Word of warning!
There's a sneeze now.
'Order, please. Now!'
Words of greeting.
Ladies' meeting!

TALKING TOGETHER

One of the most common problems in all church denominations is how to create a reverent silence before worship begins. Some churches follow solemn rituals which can create the right effect, others have a constant battle to prevent the chattering exchange of news.

It does not disturb everyone. One Minister friend was happy to see those members he knew were shut in and lonely for most of their time come alive again when they met with their friends in church.

'Talking Together' was written for one of the books of prayers published by the West Yorkshire Synod of the Methodist Church and known as WYS (pronounced 'wise') books. This prayer appeared in 'Open with God', a book containing prayers, suggestions for hymns and a selected Bible reading, all designed to be used for opening meetings – mainly women's groups. But, in order to open the meeting, the talking must stop.

LORD, we enjoy ourselves talking together.
Now we need to spend time talking to you.

We've talked about the good things that have happened:
    the exciting news from other people,
    the happy times we've shared in the past
    and all the reasons we have for looking forward.
We thank you, Lord, for the positive side of life and ask you to help us to be more
    aware of our blessings.

We've talked about unhappy things:
    those who are ill or who have died;
    the accidents and mishaps in life;
    the times when we have been upset by bad news or by the way we feel
        ourselves.
We bring these things to you now because you care about tears and fears.
Bless and comfort all those who need your care today.

We've talked about some things when we really should keep quiet:
    we've passed on that gossip overheard;
    we've judged and criticised others without knowing the truth about them;
    we've grumbled about nothing and made heavy work of our pains.
Forgive us, Lord, that we spend so much time with the negative side of life.
Teach us to look to Jesus for our example.
For although he had many reasons to be annoyed, hassled and suspicious of the
    motives of others, he reacted with humour, common sense and humility.
Show us how to live as he did, so that with your help we can make our world a
    better place.

And, as we talk again together now, may we always be aware that you are
    concerned about our conversations.

CHRISTIAN PEOPLE, SING TOGETHER

One of the great joys of discipleship is the knowledge that all Christians are part of one great family and we can find sisters and brothers everywhere. As the divisions between denominations fall, it becomes easier to worship together with a sense of unity. There will always be differences because Christians are not all alike, but trust is growing as those constant reminders that we are all part of the body of Christ begin to draw us closer together.

This hymn grew from my work with the local 'Churches Together' group, where we learned to recognise that we could not always agree upon method, but our motivation was the same.

It was first published in 'NewStart Hymns and Songs' by Kevin Mayhew Ltd, one of several books published in 1999 to be available for the millennium year. Most hymns in the book had a known tune and a new tune. In this case, the known tune was ODE TO JOY, which put my name alongside that of Ludwig van Beethoven, and the new tune was BIRCH GREEN written by Brian Hoare. For 'Multi-coloured Maze', Ian Sharp has chosen to set the text as a four-part round.

CHRISTIAN people, sing together,
all united in one voice.
Though we come from many cultures,
yet in Christ we all rejoice.
In our daily lives we're scattered,
serving God in various ways.
Then in worship we're united
giving him our thanks and praise.

God created countless faces,
yet in Christ we all are one.
Though we look from many angles,
all our views reflect the Son.
So we bring each gift and talent,
offering what we have to share,
and God blends us all together
in one body of his care.

Teach us, Lord, to trust each other,
though our ways are not the same.
As you call us to your purpose,
bless our working in your name.
In the world of daily living
each uniquely serves your will,
show how ev'ry person matters,
as our calling we fulfil.

CHRISTIAN PEOPLE (8.7.8.7.D.) *Ian Sharp (1943–)*

1. Chris - tian peo - ple, sing to - ge - ther,
2. God cre - a - ted count - less fa - ces,
3. Teach us, Lord, to trust each oth - er,

1. Though we come from ma - ny cul - tures,
2. Though we look from ma - ny ang - les,
3. As you call us to your pur - pose,

1. In our dai - ly lives we're scat - tered,
2. So we bring each gift and ta - lent,
3. In the world of dai - ly liv - ing

1. Then in wor - ship we're u - ni - ted
2. and God blends us all to - ge - ther
3. show how ev - 'ry per - son mat - ters,

(1.) all u - ni - ted in one voice.
(2.) yet in Christ we all are one.
(3.) though our ways are not the same.

(1.) yet in Christ we all re - joice.
(2.) all our views re - flect the Son.
(3.) bless our work - ing in your name.

(1.) serv - ing God in va - rious ways.
(2.) offer - ing what we have to share,
(3.) each un - ique - ly serves your will,

(1.) giv - ing him our thanks and praise.
(2.) in one bo - dy of his care.
(3.) as our call - ing we ful - fil.

WE ARE SINGING PEOPLE

The tune NOËL NOUVELET appealed to me from the first time that I sang 'Now the green blade rises' some years ago. The music demands movement and I have encouraged several groups to interpret that particular Easter carol in dance.

Inevitably I was drawn to writing my own words to this tune and this is the first of two I have written – so far. The first four words of each verse describe different aspects of our discipleship. We sing, listen, pray, work and travel, all in response to the call of Jesus.

The original text was a runner-up in the Bovingdon Hymn Competition in 1999 and has only had minor alterations made to it since then. It forms a reasonable summary of the disciple's way of life.

WE ARE singing people, bringing you our praise.
Hearts and voices lifting in our thankful days.
Joy-giving Father, in creation's song
you gave life its meaning, we will sing along.

We thank you for music and music makers
Helping us to sing your praises

We are listening people, waiting for your voice.
Seeking for your will to guide in change and choice.
Speak to us Father; make your meaning clear.
Help us base our lives upon the words we hear. *the*

Keep us listening to the for your word of your
and for the Holy Spirit sometimes spoken through others

We are praying people, seeing other's pain,
knowing there are some who dare not hope again.
Listen, dear Father, as we bring their needs.
Take our words and turn them into loving deeds.

we pray for those we know who are facing tribulation and discouragements

We are working people, each one with a task,
using time and talents, doing what you ask.
Challenge us, Father, as we hear your call,
for we are your body and you need us all.

Help us Lord to use time & talents in your service

We are travelling people, step by step with you,
for the world moves on and we must do so too.
Walk with us, Father, in our hopes and fears
and we know your love will guide us through the years.

amen

The Lord's Prayer

NOËL NOUVELET (11 11.10 11.)

Traditional French
arranged June Boyce-Tillman (1943–)

We are sing-ing peo - ple,— bring-ing— you our praise.
Hearts and voi - ces lift - ing— in our— thank-ful days.

Joy - giv-ing Fa - ther, in cre-a-tion's song—

you gave life its mean - ing,— we will— sing a - long.

Descant (optional voices or instruments)

SUPPORTIVE GOD

Many Christians work out their discipleship through voluntary organisations of all kinds. These organisations offer support and advice to those who have problems, but have no idea where to turn for help. Other disciples work full-time in this area.

Supporting others is a keynote of Christian service, one that occurs throughout this multi-coloured maze of our relationship with God and with others.

Supportive God,
through us you offer help and care
to many who have lost their connections
with what we call a 'normal' lifestyle.

Help us to seek out those for whom love is a difficult concept;
those who feel that family, or society, have failed them;
those who are caught in a cycle of trouble, or poverty, or despair
and those whose problems are beyond our understanding.

You understand and care and offer support.
Help us to see where we fit into that network.

The Family Way

Finding God in church and in worship seems to be a very natural thing to do. Finding God in family life can be fraught with difficulties. Christian families should be happy, contented and able to talk through any situation together. Or is that only in books and obituaries?

Many people find that being a Christian within the family can be the hardest part of the Christian way. Our families know us too well and are quick to point out our failings. And loving on a personal level is a joyful experience, but when things go wrong it hurts very deeply. Pain, sorrow, breaking of relationships and bereavement can create shattering experiences.

Emotions like this happen in the wider family sense too. People who have few natural relations build a family for themselves with friends, in the church or community, or in the working environment and the same joys and pains can be experienced in this wider family setting.

Much of the material in the 'Family Way' section was written originally for anthologies compiled by Geoffrey Duncan for Canterbury Press. At frequent intervals a letter arrives with detailed outlines of his next anthology and several of these have reflected on the everyday happenings of life and how we cope with them in a Christian context. Because of the personal nature of many of the experiences in this section, it is inevitable that you will discover much about my life. But those events are not unique to me and will reflect in the lives of others. Other pieces have been written as a result of situations in the lives of people whose agony or joy I have only witnessed at second hand, but these are no less real. Through them all, we learn much about God in the everyday. Also, because of the nature of this section, there are a larger proportion of prayers and poems than in the others and no dramatic pieces. Life itself is drama enough.

A BLESSING FOR A NEWBORN CHILD

We start at the very beginning. The first few days after the birth of a baby can be the most exciting, challenging and frightening hours in the life of new parents and the welcoming family. There is so much promise, but will it be fulfilled? Each baby is unique and who knows what will happen in the future?

DEAR God, there is so much potential in this small creation.
Bless this new life, that all the promise we see here is fulfilled.
Grant love, discipline and encouragement in even measures, that growth may be strong and steady.
When the learning curve dips, or experience seems too harsh a teacher, or love fails, wrap your caring arms around her/him until the weeping stops and the future begins to offer hope again.
Strengthen the love, the will and the nerve of those who will care for this young life and nourish it, for they are so aware of the weight of their responsibilities.
Help us all to see in this small scrap of humanity, so new to this world, yet another image of your many-faceted face.

NOISE

New parents will understand this poem, particularly first-time mothers. It has always brought nods of agreement when used with women's groups of all ages.

IN THE once silent night there are car doors now slamming
and motor bikes revving and garage doors banging;
and the roar of the traffic goes on till the morning,
while the birds chorus loudly as day starts its dawning.
The clock on the church nearby rings out each hour,
disturbing the bats, which squeal out from the tower.
Two cats start a serenade, screeching and wailing,
which sets a stray dog barking over the railing.
Young revellers pass, loudly shouting and singing,
and somewhere out there an alarm bell is ringing.
The wind howls forlornly and now rain is pouring;
while right there beside me my husband is snoring.
So why, in this world of sound, surging and seething,
do I only wake up when the baby stops breathing?

Although this is a common and recognisable experience, it has been pointed out that for parents whose child was a victim of 'cot death' these words may bring agonising memories. Please pray for them.

LORD, WE ASK YOU BLESS AND KEEP

One of a series of short everyday blessings based on the minor – and sometimes major – frustrations of coping with a family.

LORD, we ask you bless and keep
these dear children as they sleep.
But we ask, for our own sake,
help us cope when they're awake.

MOODS

Children are not the only ones to have mood swings, but theirs do seem to be more noticeable and possibly more frequent than any other age group. As a child, I can remember those frustrating days in the school holidays when it rained and indoor activities soon seemed very boring, as I wanted to be out with my friends. Watching the rain on the window one day reminded me of that time.

LIFE is grey
like the rain
falling on my window pane.
On the street
people stare,
no one's going anywhere.
Empty days,
nights so long.
Can't help feeling
I'm all wrong.
Life is grey.

Comes the sun,
clears the sky.
Now my spirit's
soaring high.
Lots to do
and I must go,
why is everyone so slow?
Can't they see
life is good?
Surely everybody should –
in the sun?

BLESS THE MEAL

Youngsters have very firm ideas of which foods they like and which they hate. But they are surprisingly forgiving towards the family cook and very rarely expect cordon bleu standards. Which is just as well, because few of us could reach them.

BLESS the meal upon this table,
cooked as well as I am able.
It may not have the gourmet touch,
but we'll enjoy it very much
and, if it keeps us fit and healthy,
what need have we for being wealthy?

FOR A TEENAGER'S BEDROOM

Not every teenager goes through the 'messy bedroom' stage – so they say. But judging by the reaction received for this blessing, the proportion of tidy teenagers is very small indeed.

BLESS the mess behind this door –
it's just a statement, I am sure –
that says, 'My life is all confused'
and though I may not be amused,
Lord, keep me counting up the days –
remind me this is just a phase!
And, as I love my child so much,
strengthen my will to keep in touch.

TEACHING GOD

The process of learning goes on right through life, but is intensified in schools, colleges and universities. Bringing a Christian undercurrent to that teaching, without being accused of preaching, can mean walking a tightrope of faith. All who work in education need our prayers, as do those young people who are faced with a bewildering choice of new ideas and theories.

TEACHING God,
the whole of life is a learning process,
but there are some times when our learning curve is at its highest
and our minds most receptive to new ideas.

We pray for all those who are in education –
both those who study and those who teach.
Bless those who try to incorporate Christian teaching and experience
into the educational system
and all who attempt to open minds to your truth,
for theirs is a daunting task today,
as so many people close their minds to truth.

But learning about you
is not the same as understanding you.

Eternal teacher,
keep us from the fatal mistake
of thinking that we know it all.

NEW DIRECTIONS

At certain key points in our lives major decisions have to be made. On some occasions the direction is clear and we can move forward with confidence. But many decisions make us uncertain, with opinions wavering from one side to the other, as we try to determine the best course to take. Even when the problem is resolved there is always the final moment of hesitation. Am I really doing the right thing?

LORD, I'm standing in a doorway and I don't know whether I'm coming or going.
I'm not sure whether I'm confident and happy about stepping into a new life,
or dragging my feet because I'm uneasy about leaving the old one behind.

Why did you make thresholds, Lord?
Or was that us?
And how is it that one small step can have so much significance?

I can't make it without you, Lord.
I need to remind myself of the steps you took when you were a person like me:

From your mother's care to the rabbi's teaching.
From the carpenter's shop to a wandering ministry.
From the private life to a public challenge.
From the safety of the countryside to the trials of Jerusalem.
From life on earth to death on a cross.
From the tomb to the resurrection.

Lord, what is my journey compared to yours?
But it comforts me to know that you understand my indecision.

DEAR GOD, WHEN YOU MOVE

Sometimes God seems to take matters into his own hands and we are left wondering why. It would be good to have a little warning beforehand ...

DEAR God, when you move in mysterious ways,
do you think you could warn me it's one of those days?

MOTHER OF THE GROOM

As children grow up and away to make their own lives, parents have very mixed feelings about the process. It is good to see the fulfilment of early promise and to watch as a relationship becomes a deep love, which leads to a new commitment – in this case, of a son to another woman.

Yet on the day of the wedding many other memories come flooding back.

MEMORY and time play tricks today –
I feel my arms cradling you
at the font of baptism,
weep frustrated tears at sleepless nights,
watch delighted as your eyes,
so newly opened on this world,
widen in recognition of my face.

But here I see you grown into a man –
arms cradled around the woman of your choice –
arrayed in unfamiliar elegance
and radiant with the newness of your vows.

Still I touch hot and grubby hands;
see grimy knees and shirt in disarray;
hear teenage tantrums, face dismissive stares
and answer endless questions.

Time shifts again and celebrates this day.
Take your new path with joy.
Today I gain a daughter through your love.
Add new dimensions to my memories
and look for added happiness.
Yet, child or man, you live within my heart.
Go with my love.

A WOMAN'S PLACE

In many areas of life women now have a much more prominent role to play and that is as it should be. Still there is one major area of difficulty – having a child. Women who want to marry and have children and still fulfil a career, or maintain their independence, have a constant battle between the mother instinct and the independent spirit. Where do Christian women stand on the issue? Is there an answer?
Or will it remain a constant puzzle?

WOMEN took the servant role so often –
a wife ... worth more than rubies;
watching over the affairs of her household,
not eating the bread of idleness,
fearing the Lord ... is to be praised.

And yet ...
through wombs once barren,
miracles are made.
Sarah, Hannah, Elizabeth,
played their part
in God's will brought to life.
And there was Mary,
young and fertile –
one of many who bore that name –
featuring in the good news
of God-man born of woman.

Servants still.
Obedient to the will of God,
that he might fulfil his purpose.

Or is the servanthood –
of bringing God to birth –
creative power
beyond man's understanding?
Woman's unique gift
in self-sacrifice.

In which case,
Mary's 'Let it be
according to your will' –
is not submission,
but fulfilment.

But ...
'it's all a woman's good for!'
they tell us.

BLESS THIS HOUSE

Organising time is an erratic occupation. It is always possible to find time for the things we want to do, but there are others that get pushed to the side.

> BLESS this house and all that's in it –
> it would be clean, if I had a minute!
> But really Lord, most folk don't mind –
> it's friendship they come here to find.

A BLESSING FOR THOSE WITH AUTHORITY

Some jobs are extremely stressful. Perhaps the worst of these are experienced by those who have to administer authority in some way and yet have no power to change the rules that govern the work they have to do. This can make them very unpopular, as they are perceived as inflexible and hard-hearted. Indeed, if they are constantly interpreted as being the enemy, it can lead to a certain unwilling hardening of the attitude, if only for self-protection.

These people need our prayers, because so many of them really are misunderstood. And, yes, I did work in an unpopular department of a Local Authority!

UNDERSTANDING God, we ask your blessing on all those whose work demands that they wear the mask of authority, for that can create fear, hostility and misunderstanding.

Bless those who work for governments, national and local, especially when they have to develop unpopular policies.

Bless those who work in tax and benefit offices, or who deal with housing, or problems of social deprivation; especially when they are faced with situations that they cannot officially help to resolve.

Bless those whose work is to enforce the law by policing, or in court, or prison for they face hatred, violence and hostility on a daily basis.

Bless those whose authority is seen to be petty officialdom by many people; traffic wardens, bank managers, doctors' receptionists, ticket inspectors and the many others whose daily working life brings them into contact with an uncooperative public, for they so often have to cope with the backlash of frustration.

Bless all those who often wonder why they should have to suffer so much hostility simply because they are doing their job. Save them from becoming hardened and cynical and hostile themselves. Reaffirm the positive aspects of their work and grant them endless patience.

Comfort them with the knowledge that Jesus counted a tax collector among his closest friends.

HAPPINESS IS LIKE ...

Happiness is not always an obvious state. Sometimes it just creeps up on us from our everyday experiences. It weaves a web around us, but the threads are delicate and easily broken.

HAPPINESS is like a spider's web made up of delicate threads leading off in
    different directions.
To family, friends and people we meet by chance.
To activities we enjoy and everyday pleasures of home, meals, warmth and food.
To the created world and the creative spirit in us.
To music and words that cheer our spirits.
To fun and laughter and the joy of a bright day.

All these threads are connected and circled by the love of those around us
    and your love is at the centre, Lord.
This web of happiness is strong, but it can be destroyed by harsh treatment
    and the storms of life.

Yet Lord, while we live and you live in us, the pattern can be recreated,
    because nothing can separate your love from us.

That promise of yours is the source of our joy and the origin of all those
    delicate threads of love.

Thank you, Lord.

DEPRESSION

Depression can also start in small ways, hardly noticeable, yet insidiously creeping up and becoming overpowering in their effect. As full-blown depression strikes, it becomes impossible to believe that anyone understands, or cares. Even God.

O GOD, where are you?
I can't get through to you any more!
Why doesn't anyone understand the way I'm feeling?
I can't do anything right.
Everyone is ignoring my problems and the state I'm in.
I don't seem to matter to anyone, but I can't cope on my own.
I can't carry on like this!
I'm either going to start shouting and screaming to make people listen,
or I'll shut myself off from the lot of them.
They don't care, anyway!

But I thought you did, Lord! Why can't I get through to you?

*(Jesus on the cross cried out, 'My God, my God, why have you abandoned me?'
His prayer was answered in the resurrection. So is ours.)*

TEMPTATION

'Lead us not into temptation', we say, in the most commonly used version of the Lord's Prayer. But do we mean it? Or are there reservations? Are there areas of life where we are happy to give in to temptation, because that is the course we really want to take?

God is not responsible for us making fools of ourselves, if we are not prepared to listen to him. Experience is usually the best teacher and having to face the consequences of our self-willed behaviour can have a devastating, but memorable, effect.

How could I have been such a fool, Lord?
It was so easy to convince myself that there was nothing wrong.
With temptation staring me in the face –
and easily identifiable –
I still gave in.

How lame my excuses were.
'If God doesn't want me to do this,
then he'll stop me.'
As if you would, Lord!
How could I not see that sometimes you make sure
we learn by our mistakes –
the hard way?
'It can't be bad, if it feels so right.'
The answer to that one is there
at the beginning of the Bible.
What else are we supposed to learn
from the story of Adam and Eve?
'No one who knows me will ever find out.'
And what happened when they did?
Shock. Disbelief. Hurt. Despair.
It took so long to put things right again.
And *you* knew all the time!

But I have learned my lesson, Lord,
and will not make *that* mistake again,
I promise.
Forgive me, please,
even though I'm finding it hard to forgive myself.
And I know that there will be new temptations
just around the corner –
and I am only human –
but keep me alert,
so that I may not fall for the plausible excuse
every time.

AFTER MARRIAGE BREAKDOWN

My marriage is strong, although there have been rough patches along the way. But I have seen the marriages of friends break down and have been drawn into the tears and pain by a concern for their welfare.

Each marriage is unique and each breakdown is different, but heartache and heart-searching are always present and learning to live with failure is never easy.

OH, GOD, now my marriage has ended.
It is over –
and I must face the fact that vows made before you
and other witnesses
have been broken beyond repair.
There has been hurt and recrimination
and shock and much heart-searching.
There have been many tears.
But now the parting is real
and I must deal with it.

Could things have worked out differently?
Only you know that.

But I must live today –
and all the tomorrows –
in different circumstances now.
There is so much pain,
but I must move on.

Go with me, Lord,
and help me to learn from this harrowing experience.
Forgive me for the part that I have played
in allowing this to happen.
Show me how to deal with memories that flood my mind
at unexpected times
and bring tears, or laughter, or regrets.
Teach me to root out bitterness
as if it were an invasive weed,
otherwise it will grow and flourish
and choke all positive thought
and any chance of new growth.
Take me by the hand
and lead me through the rough paths of building new relationships.
Touch me with your love
in those desolate moments
when I must learn
to take the burden of my loneliness away
from long-suffering friends.
Restore my confidence Lord,
and help me to put my life back together again.

LIVES HAVE BEEN BROKEN

Attending a weekend conference on creative worship, we were given one session in which to 'do our own thing'. The previous week I had been looking at the hymn 'Morning has broken' and examining its unusual rhyming scheme, so I decided to try to write my own piece to this pattern. The theme of broken relationships was on my mind as I had heard recent news of a difficult and disruptive situation that had arisen in a church and recognised that many people had been deeply hurt. But the words of this hymn could apply equally well to any broken relationship.

Because I was following the 'Morning has broken' rhyming scheme, the piece was originally written to the tune BUNESSAN. Perhaps that tune is so strong that the words will not fit any other tune comfortably. Or perhaps someone will prove me wrong about that one day.

LIVES have been broken. Peace has been shattered.
Words have been spoken best left unsaid.
Lying around us, remnants of loving.
Joy out of focus, happiness dead.

Careless of feeling, trampling onwards –
barely concealing lack of concern –
hurting and bleeding follow our actions.
Where is it leading? When will we learn?

Stark and revealing, comes that dark moment,
when broken feeling makes us aware.
All we have shattered, all we have broken,
loving that mattered, no longer there.

Then comes the sorrow. Realisation!
What of tomorrow? Torment, remorse!
Lord, grant us healing in our awareness,
your love revealing compassion's source.

Lord, take our sadness. Grant us renewal.
Out of this madness, help us to see,
as we rebuild life and beg forgiveness,
we find your new life setting us free.

BUNESSAN (10.9.10.9.)

Traditional Gaelic
arranged Craig McLeish (1963–)

Lives have been bro - ken. Peace has been shat - tered. Words have been spo - ken best left un - said. Ly-ing a - round us, rem - nants of lov - ing. Joy out of fo - cus, hap - pi - ness dead.

A BLESSING FOR A NEW START

When a bad experience is over it is best to put it away in the past and move on. That is what Christian repentance, forgiveness and renewal are all about. God knows that if we hold on to our hates and grievances they will only fester and poison the rest of our lives. He offers us a way to move on, but we must take those positive steps ourselves.

FACE the future
for the past is over and gone.
Live with the memories.
Learn from experience.
Let go of grievances.
Resolve differences.
Live in the sight of God
in the way of God. ·
Be strong.
He has seen us through
good times and bad.
He will bless our future
as he has held our past.

God go with you.

HAPPINESS – MOUNTAIN TOPS

A new start can give an injection of hope and happiness, although unpleasant memories sometimes come without warning. Yet we can learn from every experience, if we are prepared to do so.

THANK you, Lord, that today I have been on the mountain tops,
but help me to recognise that valleys are beautiful too –
even if they are more often in the shadow.

FOR SOMEONE WITH LEARNING DIFFICULTIES

When I was a child we had Albert living next door to us. He was known to everyone as 'the big daft lad', a north-eastern expression that seemed harmless enough at the time, but would make sensitive people shudder today. He had severe learning difficulties, but nothing much was ever done to help him and he was frequently taunted by local children and misunderstood by adults.

Thankfully, today things have changed, and people with learning difficulties are given special attention and helped to live and work as independently as they can. But there is still misunderstanding and people can be dismissive and unhelpful.

Are we not all made in the image of God?

FATHER, hold this child of yours
who has difficulty in understanding
everyday things that come so easily to others.

May this life be blessed
by a supportive family,
loving carers,
patient teachers,
understanding friends
and helpful strangers.

Open the eyes of those who are cruel,
deliberately, or thoughtlessly;
so that they are able to see
your image in this life
as much as in any other.

Reach out with your deep joy
which goes beyond understanding
and your love, which has no limits,
but speaks heart to heart;
so that your child
can know the wonder
of being a member of your family.

HEALING GOD

The concept of Christian healing can create great difficulties for certain groups of people. There are Christians who imply that healing prayer always works and, if it doesn't, then the person does not have enough faith.

This is at best an unthinking attitude to take and it can be very cruel to those for whom there is no cure for their problem.

HEALING God, reach out to the lives
of those who are sick in mind or body.
Medical science does not have the solutions to all problems,
so we pray especially for those people for whom no cure can be found.

Comfort and sustain them
as they cope with their problems
and give them your peace in their darkest times.
Help those who are with them –
relatives, friends, carers and medical staff –
to be strong in their support and compassionate in their care,
even though they too are under great stress.

Teach us to see life from their perspective
and to be alert to their particular needs.

LIGHTHOUSE – MEMORIAL

A friend who is a Methodist Minister used his sabbatical time to work in London with groups who were caring for victims of HIV/AIDS. Part of his time was spent at the Lighthouse, a centre set up by AIDS sufferers and their supporters, to offer medical care, counselling and support.

During the time that Robert worked there I attended a weekend event in London and asked if I could see something of the work he was doing, as I was a member of his sabbatical support group. Robert took me to see the public areas at the Lighthouse project, I met one or two of the people there and then he took me into the Memorial Room.

At this point I knew little about the AIDS problem, other than it was mainly confined to the gay community at that time. Certainly I had not understood how uncaring the church had been towards the problem. Robert explained how the Memorial Room had been set up to provide a substitute for the care and attention that should have been given by the churches to those sufferers and their families.

It was a large, plain room with one wall filled with a huge photograph taken at a rally in a London park. Some of the faces on the photograph were circled – they had died of AIDS. On a long table were books containing photographs and tributes written by partners, friends or families. Page after page was filled with sorrow and celebration. The other walls were filled with banners, each commemorating a life that meant so much to those who created them.

It was the dates on those banners that finally shattered my indifference. My son was in his mid-twenties at the time and almost every date showed that the victim who had died was younger than him.

Suddenly the grief and agony in that room totally overwhelmed me. It was as if all those hurting people were crowding around me and I was being slowly suffocated by their pain. Robert took my arm and led me to the quiet room. I was so ashamed that my indifference could be interpreted as being part of the uncaring attitude of the church.

That night I couldn't sleep – until, at two in the morning, I began to pour out those feelings on paper.

ONLY an empty room,
four walls, a floor, a ceiling.
But hard-pressed into that place –
what feeling!

Crowd scene up on a wall,
pictured in nameless meeting.
But, life for some shadowed face –
how fleeting!

Banners in colours bright,
beauty and passion blended.
Only the dates tell the tale –
life ended!

Careless, to gaze I came,
but what a weight of sorrow
burdens my troubled memory
tomorrow – and tomorrow – and tomorrow!

CONFUSION

When Geoffrey Duncan asked me to contribute to his anthology of worship material to 'allow gay, lesbian, bisexual and transgender men and women to affirm their sexuality', I thought very carefully before responding to his request. Although the experience at the Lighthouse had made me look at this community in a different way, I still had difficulty in reconciling this with my more traditional beliefs that the heterosexual way of life was the right one. Working with young people for years, I was also concerned that many were being asked to decide on their sexuality, at a time when their emotions and sex drive were so high that they were in a confused state of mind anyway. The recent trauma of a marriage break-up by friends, because of this problem, was also still very fresh in my mind.

I believe this state of confusion is common to many Christians and Geoffrey allowed me to express this, as he recognised that others would feel the same way about the subject.

BLACK and white,
once innocent,
now politically incorrect.
Male and female,
clear-cut
no longer.
Right and wrong,
edges blurred
by genetics, environment,
psychology.
Values and norms,
absorbed in childhood,
fuelled by faith,
overturned by change.

Help me, Lord,
blundering through
new moral mazes,
to tread lightly
in areas strange to me
and to speak softly
in unfamiliar surroundings.

Keep my mind open, Lord,
to possibilities
not yet considered
and, when acceptance is difficult,
keep me loving
beyond my reason.

LISTENING GOD

Another hymn written to the tune NOËL NOUVELET.

There are times when God seems to be keeping his distance. Times when situations overwhelm us, grief is too great to bear, depression and desperation have set in, or life has become removed from God, as our own interests and concerns take precedence over everything else. God seems so far away that he cannot be reached and we are so lost in our misery that we have no energy left to find him.

It is reassuring to know that, when the heaviness has lifted, God is waiting patiently for us to recognise him again.

LISTENING God, you hear us when we cannot speak,
when despair and turmoil leave us faint and weak.
In love you call us back to you again
and your grace reminds us how you feel our pain.

Searching God, you find us when we go astray,
as self-centred living takes us from your way.
In love you seek us, show us what we've lost,
and your tears remind us what forgiveness cost.

Suffering God, you lift us from our deepest grief,
when emotion blinds us to our own belief.
In love you touch us with your nail-torn hand
and your wounds remind us why you understand.

Risen God you show us love too strong for death.
Evil deeds defeated by your living breath.
In love you teach us never to despair,
your new life reminds us, hope is always there.

NOËL NOUVELET (11 11.10 11.)

Traditional French
arranged Peter Cutts (1937–)

Listen-ing God, you hear us when we__ can-not speak,
when des-pair and tur-moil leave us__ faint and weak.

In love you call us back to you a - gain

and your grace re - minds us how you__ feel our pain.

FATHER, I MAY NOT BE ....

Singing is not one of my strong points, although singing together as Christians can be a very exhilarating experience. There is inspiration in music and sometimes it can make all the difference to the day.

FATHER, I may not be much of a singer, but today I caught the spirit of your song
and it inspired me to sing along with you.
Thank you for all the beauty and the energy and the vitality of the music of your
creative power and your love.
Teach me how to be in tune with you more often, because it is a wonderful feeling
to have something to sing about.

NOT KNOWING ANYONE

Shy people know the agony of entering a room full of strangers and feeling terrified at having to be the one to start a conversation. Bravado can help, but it doesn't always work. Pretending to be someone else – although only to yourself – also has its merits. But, best of all, is if someone recognises you.

ALONE,
and just inside that crowded room,
I stood,
the Babel-babble conversation
roaring round me.
But I was edgy and bewildered,
unconnected.

Until, across the room
I heard my name –
not called,
but spoken of with knowledge –
and there was one, at least,
who recognised my being,
not my face.

It was enough.
Existing in her mind
she had enlivened me.
Now I could be part
of those around.

I wonder –
did that woman ever know
how she had spoken me to life?

TOUCHING

The sense of touch is a God-given gift. We know the pleasure of stroking the fur of an animal, or cuddling a teddy bear! All around us there are textures to examine with our fingers – tree bark, flower petals, cool water, silky fabrics, rough wool, smooth stone, warm wood – the list is endless.

But making human contact by touch is something very different. There are people who will hug anyone in sight, but there are also those who avoid even a handshake – and telling them apart is not always easy. It is wise to be wary until the personality of the person is revealed.

Yet Jesus was constantly reaching out to touch people, to heal them and to reassure them. How do we safely follow his example?

God of all our senses, so many people were touched by your love
through the hands of Jesus as he healed and helped them in his lifetime.
A blind man felt spittle on his eyelids.
A leper felt long-forgotten human connection.
A young girl was given new life as Jesus helped her to her feet.
A woman was healed as she reached out in desperation for his robe.
We sometimes forget what healing power there can be in the sense of touch.

Loving God, we ask a special blessing on those who never feel the friendly touch
of someone who cares for them –
those who live alone and are anxious about making contact with others;
those who suffer physical abuse from people they should be able to trust;
those who keep themselves apart and have forgotten how to be friendly;
those who can only respond to others with distrust and anger;
those whose relationship with their partner is breaking down,
and especially those who once enjoyed a close, loving relationship with a
partner who has now died, for they have known the everyday warmth of love
and face a special emptiness.

Healing God, touch the lives of those suffering from anxiety, abuse, isolation,
anger, broken relationships or bereavement.
Teach us to know when it would be appropriate to offer a hand to shake or hold,
or the eye contact that signifies trust.
We are sometimes too wary of reaching out to offer your hand of healing.
Help us to imagine ourselves into the other person's shoes,
so that with your guidance we can offer patience, friendship and a genuine loving
concern to all who need your care.

LOSS OF SIGHT

Losing one of the senses that have become a familiar part of life can be a devastating experience. My mother became increasingly deaf as she aged, and her major frustration was the telephone. Even with an adaptor fitted to the handset, there were times when she still could not hear me using my loudest voice – and I am capable of silencing a room in seconds, if it is necessary to do so!

My husband is now registered as partially-sighted and even close friends do not always understand what anxieties that can create.

How useless I feel, Lord,
now that I can no longer see properly.

For me there are no more eyes meeting across a crowded room,
no more sideways glances to convey intimacy,
no more sharing the joke by the twitch of the lips,
no more reading the truth by the averted gaze,
no more recognising a friend from a distance.

Now I stand alone
waiting for the sensitive ones
to identify themselves and engage me –
while others wonder why I never speak
to them.
Little do they know
how often I thought I did,
only to embarrass a stranger.

Lord, it is so hard,
when I have grown accustomed to the seeing world,
to find myself no longer there.

Help me to persevere
in finding ways of coping.
Help me to be patient
in my dealings with those who do not understand.
Console me in my loss of dignity
and in my reluctance to be dependent on others.
Restore the soul of my independence,
by teaching me new ways of self-reliance
and by using skills which are not affected
by my sight-impairment,
to be of service to others.

Lord, my life is still yours.
Help me to follow this confusing direction
with hope and confidence in You.

THE TELEPHONE

Living alone, the telephone can be a lifeline to the outside world. It is another of those blessings that many of us take for granted.

BLESS, dear Lord, my telephone.
With it, I am not alone.
Though some callers are a pest,
I'll look forward to the rest.
Friends and family sounding near –
voices that I love to hear.
And, when people need my time,
keep me, Lord, upon the line.

SOLITUDE

The person at the other end of the telephone line may feel a little differently about the interruption when it rings, but recognises the need and responds to it.
Sometimes solitude can be a blessing, but not for everyone.

JUST when I get a moment to myself
the phone rings
and I hear the voice
I know so well.
I also know
that time will soon be flying.

But loneliness,
not an issue for me,
is hard for her –
and keeping me a little longer
on the line
puts off the moment
of the single cup of tea
and listless
staring at the television set.

Solitude is not a state
wished for by everyone.

RETIREMENT

There are those who embrace retirement from work with open arms. They throw themselves enthusiastically into all those areas of interest which they have not had time to pursue while they were working and, within a matter of weeks, they wonder how they ever had time to work at all.

Others find the situation much more difficult. Their work may have been their whole life and a very fulfilling experience. Or perhaps there is some physical reason which prevents them from being as active as they used to be.

They need God's care and concern administered through Christian compassion.

Now I am retired, who am I?

Once I had status,
the satisfaction of a job well done.
Colleagues formed a colony,
and we were comfortable in our world.
The days were busy,
too much so, at times;
but there was pattern, structure
and a motive to the day.

Now that sense of purpose is no more.
No reason why anyone should consult me,
talk to me,
or ask me how the day has gone.

I'm lost –
and this strange world of nothingness
stretches before me,
except for eating and sleeping and being entertained.
Knowledge, skills, experience –
all in the past.

Unless you can find a new use for them, Lord?

THROUGH ALL THE CHANGING SCENES

Thankfully, the ageing process creeps up so gradually that it comes as a great shock to look in the mirror one day and see the image of a parent staring back.

Other people only see this outer image and have no way of judging how old any other person really feels. Some of the ninety-and-over group that I know would surprise you if you ever asked them their inner age.

But time flies – no matter how old, or young, you are.

Five! Alive! Now see me go!
Splash through raindrops, stomp through snow.
Life's for living – finding out
what my world is all about.

Twenty-five! My path is clear.
I know where I'll be next year.
Future perfect. Partner picked.
Look out life! I've got you licked!

Forty-five! Safe and secure.
No longer brash and immature.
Healthy, happy, unconcerned.
I'm enjoying what I've earned.

Sixty-five! Retired at last!
Life was getting far too fast!
Now my time is all my own –
can't believe how fast it's flown.

Eighty-five! Can this be me?
My mirror tells me what you see.
My secret life the glass will hide –
I'm still a five-year-old inside!

A BLESSING FOR SOMEONE WITH ALZHEIMER'S DISEASE

Not all eighty-five-year-olds are aware of how young or old they feel. Dementia, or Alzheimer's Disease, can rob an otherwise healthy person of all contact with normal human life. They are not always aware of their condition, but it is a painful process for those who watch this disintegration and can do little to help.

At the time this piece was written a friend's husband had recently been diagnosed with the disease. When there is nothing else you can do to help someone you love, you can always pray.

LORD, we ask your blessing on this confused mind.
You know that the experiences and knowledge of a lifetime are locked away
    inside a complicated mechanism to which this disease has inappropriate keys.

Keep this troubled one safe in confusion,
happy in forgetfulness,
aware in times of lucidity
and secure in the environment of constant care.

When there is fear and anger, surround her/him with your peace.
When despair strikes, give her/him your glimmer of hope.
When there seems to be no response, probe deep into the apparent emptiness of
    the mind with the reassurance of your love.

And when everything seems hopeless and this disease has full control, we commit
    her/him to your eternal compassion and care.

Amen

ECHOES

This was written from my own family's experience of the same disease.

My mother's sister was known to all as 'Nan', because I had difficulty in coping with the name 'Auntie Annie' as a small child. She had shared most of my life and was 'my other mother' to me. When she was almost ninety she had to go into a nursing home and we travelled the eighty miles to see her about once a month. But Alzheimer's Disease took control of her and confusion and frustration led first to irrational behaviour, then to emptiness. Very occasionally something would break through from the past and Nan would be there again. But not often.

When the 'Methodist Recorder' announced 'Living Words' as the theme for its 2002 poetry competition, this incident seemed to produce its own echoes of reality. The poem was one of the runners-up in the competition that year. More importantly, it has proved to be the source of tears, and yet comfort, to others whose relatives or friends have suffered in the same way.

CONFUSED, alone, she sat,
not deep in the chair, but on the edge of it.
Her fingers twisting in an endless circle
of emptiness.
Eyes seeing nothing we could follow.
Mind in a distant place beyond our reach.
No flicker of recognition or welcome
from the one who had cradled me,
nurtured me, waited eagerly for my step
inside the door each day.

Words were no use, we thought.
This was a bad day
and she would never know we had been there
watching the disintegration
of her fiery, independent spirit;
the slow loss –
although today she was gone from us already.

Elsewhere rustles of interest
told the arrival of the keyboard player
with tattered books of music
from a bygone age
and those who could, gathered in chattering flock
to finger-tap and listen.

And then, among melodies familiar with age,
came 'bright and beautiful' and 'creatures great and small',
and a thin, clear voice from that lonely chair
joined in a chorus from some childhood time.
Life gave its echo back to us
and brought the tears.

CARING GOD

*Christians are called to care about others, but it is not always easy to know how to
fulfil that calling. Sympathy is a starting point, but getting alongside the sufferer is
so much better, although a much more demanding course of action.*

A willingness to serve is essential, but patience and endurance are also needed.

CARING God,
your heart goes out to those who suffer
and we must reach out too.

But it is not an easy thing to get alongside someone
and feel their suffering with them.
It takes endless patience and time and energy
and we cannot always sustain the effort.

Keep us loving beyond the limits that we believe are possible,
for your care goes further than we can ever imagine
into the darkest places of suffering, grief and despair.

COMFORTER – A HYMN FOR CARERS

*There are many people caring for relatives or friends who are ill or frail, either
because they feel it is their duty to do so, or because their love is so strong that there
really is no other option.*

*But even the most dedicated of carers have their own needs too, and the stress
and strain of loving concern can be so overwhelming that it leads to resentment and
frustration.*

*When it becomes evident that the suffering can only end in death, then the
emotions are in turmoil. Having to watch the prolonged disintegration of a loved
one can lead to all kinds of questions and doubts. Should this life be prolonged? Is
there no other way? Why, Lord? And when?*

*All we can do is to turn to a God who understands our distress and supports us
with his love.*

WHEN our caring love wears thin,
when our nerves are stretched and taut
and the strain of our concern
fills our every waking thought –
God of understanding heart,
give us strength to play our part.

When we watch in helpless love
when all hope of health is past
and distress cries out in pain
that this suffering will not last –
God of healing, hold us near,
bring your calm and drive out fear.

When our tears speak out our love,
when by smiles we mask our grief,
in those dark and lonely hours
when the silence mocks belief –
God of comfort, to our night
bring the dawning of your light.

When the one we loved has gone,
when death brings tormented peace,
as emotions swirl around,
sorrow mingled with release –
God of patience, bear our pain;
turn us back to life again.

The last verse may be omitted if inappropriate.

GOD OF COMFORT (7.7.7.7.7 7.)

Ian Sharp (1943–)

With feeling

When our car - ing love wears thin, when our nerves are stretched and taut and the strain of our con - cern fills our ev - ery wak - ing thought – God of un - der - stand - ing heart, give us strength to play our part.

Optional postlude

ENDINGS

When tragedy strikes and a sudden death occurs, it can seem like the end of everything.

Why has this happened? Where was God? What's the point of going on with anything? Why here? Why now? What have we done to deserve this?

All plans for a normal future are now shattered and the emptiness and desolation can be overpowering.

But is it the end?

'THIS is the end,'
said Moses
as he saw the Red Sea cross his path,
a barrier to freedom.
And yet today
the Jews still celebrate their crossing
as a turning point
within their history.

'This is the end,'
said Elijah
hiding in his mountain cave,
cowering from danger.
And yet, from there,
through howling wind and storming rain
he saw God's power
within the stillness.

'This is the end,'
said Mary
bent with sorrow at the cross's foot
where hung her son.
And yet she heard
'Take care of her,' and felt his love
surround her even then
within the arms of John.

'This is the end,'
said Jesus
as his tortured body gave itself to death
and darkness fell.
And yet he knew
this end was but a new beginning.
No power of Rome or Jew could keep the love of God
within a tomb.

'This is the end,'
we say
when life is torn apart
by tragic loss.
And yet, beyond our grief,
the pain-filled eyes of a Father,
whose Son faced death too soon,
are weeping with us.

THIS IS THE PLACE

Although I have written all kinds of material all my life, I had never considered that any of it was worthy of a wider audience than that for which it was created. In the 1970s and '80s, I wrote Christian pieces for local radio and began to realise that this 'wider audience' was accepting my writing. But it was only when Stainer & Bell began to produce the periodical 'Worship Live' in 1994 that I seriously considered submitting my pieces for editorial judgement. From the very beginning my material was welcomed, I received constructive criticism and helpful suggestions, and I knew that I had found a fresh outlet for the gift that God had given me.

Each 'Worship Live' periodical gives details of the themes for future issues and invites material to be submitted for consideration. The first one I tackled was 'funerals and shrines' – quite a challenge for writing to a theme set by an editor who was unknown to me at that time.

Funerals are naturally surrounded by sorrow and loss and yet there is comfort in the formality of saying goodbye and the surroundings in which that takes place can be very important. That is why many who never enter a church at any other time will do so at the time of a death.

We all reach out to God when we need him most – even if we are not too sure that he is there.

This is the place
where death meets life,
where sorrow is present,
where hard questions are asked
and not always answered.

This is the place
where pain is felt,
where partings are made real,
where holy words
can ring empty and hollow.

This is the place
where we ask, 'Why?'
Where we cry, 'What now?'
Where God is near,
or feels so far away.

This is the place
where emotions are mixed,
where tears are shed,
where memories return
of brighter yesterdays.

This is the place
where God says, 'I know.'
Where God says, 'I am here.'
Where God sheds a tear
along with us.

This is the place
where God understands,
where God stands and waits,
where Jesus says,
'I went through it.'

This is the place
where Easter is hope,
where eternity is God,
where each ending
becomes a beginning.

This is the place
where God is all around
and very much alive
because we need him
here in this place.

HERE IN THIS PLACE

LONDONDERRY (11.10.11.10.11.10.11.12.)

Traditional Irish
arranged June Boyce-Tillman (1943–)

Here in this place we meet with you in sor - row, our hearts and minds with me - mo - ries are filled. We fear to face our emp - ti - ness to - mor - row, when thoughts are sad and ma - ny tears are spilled. And yet we know Lord, you have told us clear - ly that where you

Here in this place we meet with you in sorrow,
our hearts and minds with memories are filled.
We fear to face our emptiness tomorrow,
when thoughts are sad and many tears are spilled.
And yet we know Lord, you have told us clearly
that where you are, there also we will be.
You came to bring a hope of life eternal,
a promise of a future joy we cannot see.

Here in this place we gather in thanksgiving
for all we shared, the joyful days gone by;
for those we love, our chosen life's companions
and those who care and hold us when we cry.
And Lord, we know that you will take the future,
that you will walk beside us in the way
to take us on, to make a new beginning,
to comfort, guide and keep us as we face each day.

Around the time this hymn was written I had attended several funerals of older Christian friends, where the cremation had taken place with only the family present and then they had returned to church to join with the wider congregation in a service celebrating the life of the one who had died. Although these celebrations can be joyful occasions, when happy and positive memories are stirred, I felt great sympathy for those non-Christian members of the family or congregation, for whom this was only a sorrowful event.

This hymn attempts to capture those mixed emotions and to remind us of the promise of God that he will always be with us, whatever the future may hold.

A BLESSING IN BEREAVEMENT

When emotions are raw at the time of a bereavement we need to be able to rely on those around us. God uses those people to reach out with comfort and consolation.

MAY God bless you and be with you in this time of deep sorrow.

In the tears of others, know that he weeps with you.

In the touch of others, know that his arms are holding you.

In the practical work of others, know that he is helping you to cope from day to day.

In the words of others, know that he is speaking to you.

In the prayers of others, know that he hears you.

And in the desolation of this time, know that by each tear, touch, act, word and prayer, others are bringing God's love to you to filter into those empty spaces with his compassion and understanding.

The Global Way

Many of my grandparents' generation lived within twenty miles of the sea, yet were never able to stroll on the beach or take the sea air, because those twenty miles presented an insurmountable barrier to them. Now I live in a seaside town and fly to other countries on holiday and know that other people my age are even more adventurous in their travel than I am.

The world seems to have expanded and shrunk at the same time, as air travel both stretches our horizons and brings everything closer in a strange kind of double act.

If the earth is bigger than previous generations thought and yet more accessible than they could ever have believed, what difference does that make to our understanding of God as creator and sustainer of the universe? And what new attitude does that give to our Christian calling?

This section of the book contains pieces on the delights and responsibilities of our stewardship of the earth. There are items on the exploitation of the earth's resources, the use of money, injustice, poverty, war and peace. Looking at the world in this global way encourages us to see our planet as God does, as one independent entity of which we are only a small but influential part.

CREATION – A RESPONSIVE PRAYER

When writing a prayer about creation it is difficult not to be drawn into the debate between those who believe implicitly in the Biblical creation stories and those who stand firmly on the ground of the theory of evolution – and if you think that such a debate was over long ago, try writing to a newspaper about it and stand well back from the resulting postbag! Within my own mind I can reconcile the two opinions, although I sometimes find myself questioning the evolution theory along the lines of 'if creatures evolved to cope with new environments, then why so many varieties in the same place?' or 'are new species still developing and, if so, why don't we hear more about it?'

No answers, thank you! These are purely rhetorical questions.

Three elements are essential for life on earth to continue – light, water and air. All three are present in sufficient quantity to sustain life, unless we humans upset the balance by our unthinking actions. Christians believe that people are part of our creator God's creativity and that he has now left his creation in our hands.

How are we coping with that responsibility?

CREATION began with light:
light breaking through, spilling out, flooding over,
light giving illumination, warmth and energy,
light drawing life from the earth, stimulating growth.

Forgive us, Lord, for the way in which we cut off your supply of light to others by our
       careless use of energy,
our clouds of pollution and smoke screens of destruction.
Teach us that we block out the light at our peril, for light is the source of life itself.

Creation was baptised with water.
Streams and rivers, lakes and seas, brought refreshment and vitality.
Every form of life was filled out and nourished, sustained by moisture.
Rainforests dripped with it,
deserts thirsted for it,
people thrived on it.

Forgive us, Lord, that we are not careful enough with this life-giving source.
Give us a concern for those who try to exist where there is no easy access to water.
Challenge us to support research into the problem
and to care for those who suffer from it.
Teach us that the earth developed its own conservation and distribution system
       and we create danger when we disturb the balance of nature.

Creation caught its breath from your Spirit.
The earth filled its lungs with freshness.
People, plants and animals felt the stirring of the breeze.
The wind moved with force and power.

Forgive us, Lord, that we contaminate the air we breathe by our unheeding use of
pollutants.
Teach us to be selective and knowledgeable and concerned about the substances we use.
Make us more aware that moving the problem somewhere else is not the right solution.

Creation is sustained by us.

Help us, Lord, to be careful keepers of all the life sources you have given to us,
so that your creative processes may be continued in us.

SPRING – SUMMER – AUTUMN – WINTER

One of the wonderful things about living in England – and, yes, it does apply to the
rest of the United Kingdom – is that we usually have identifiable seasons of the
year. These can become blurred at the edges occasionally – snow in August is not
entirely unknown – but spring is fresh, summer is warmer, autumn is colourful
and winter is cold, all approximately in the right months of the year.

These four pieces were written for Geoffrey Duncan's anthology 'A World of
Blessing'. They are half poem, half prayer and wholly intended to focus the mind on
the blessings of the variety of the seasons of the year.

Spring

SPRING is full of energy –
like its name.
It coils and tenses and waits
and then jumps out at us,
bursting with vigour
and new life
and shouts its presence
with a this-is-what-you've-been-waiting-for attitude.

Spring blesses us in an aggressive way.
Bare trees suddenly thrusting out new leaves.
Flowers shaking their defiant colours,
even at the occasional return of wintry weather.
Animals and birds proudly parade young ones.
Lawns and hedges cry out for mowers and trimmers.
And the sun gains strength and length of days
and by its energy
urges us to get out and do something.

Energetic God,
we thank you for the urgent message of renewal
that blesses us with each spring.

Summer

SUMMER is extravagant
and overstated
and showy.

Summer colours are bright
and gaudy
and over-the-top.

Summer life is abundant
and prolific
and overwhelming.

Summer sun is dazzling
and brilliant
and hot –

sometimes.

Summer rain is warmer,
but just as wet
as at any other time.

Yet summer riots its colours loudest
where sun and showers combine
to bring out the glory.

Just as God's blessings abound
in the joy and sorrow
by which all growth comes.

Autumn

AUTUMN is a blazing time,
a red and gold amazing time.
Trees maturing now display
fruit and leaf in fine array.
Trees prepared for winter's rest
show their glories at their best.

Autumn is a dying time,
a withering and a drying time.
Falling leaves are brittle rust
tumbling down into the dust.
Fallen leaves go back to earth,
re-absorbed to bring new birth.

Autumn is a blessing time,
a God-will-keep-us-guessing time.
Emptying branches seem so stark,
stripped to bare and simple bark.
Empty branches on them bear
sleeping buds to wake next year.

Winter

Winter has a dreary sound to it.
Fog, frost, snow, rain and icy winds
all feature heavily.
They turn us indoors
to layers of warm clothing
and firesides and hot drinks,
which are all blessings in themselves.

But on bright winter days
there are unexpected joys.
Sunshine on snow.
Sparkling frosty air.
Tree outlines silhouetted by clear blue sky.
And piercing through the hardened soil
the sharp green points of new life.

We know it will always happen,
but it is good to see
God blessing us, once again,
with his promise of resurrection.

AMAZING GOD

As Christians we are called to widen our horizons from our own self-contained world and to look at the larger global issues, because earth is a fragile planet needing our care and attention, as do the people who share this world with us, however far or near they may be.

Amazing God, your world is vast and wide
and we are only a very small part of it.
Yet our world, however small, expands to fill our whole horizon
and encloses us within it
to keep us contained and comfortable.
Open our eyes to larger visions
and to the way that all our lives interconnect
in a world which appears to grow smaller by the minute.
We are all your family, wherever we are.

CREATIVE CARELESSNESS

Having watched yet another doom-laden television programme about the pollution of the planet, the changing shape of the ozone layer and the decimation of the rainforests, I then looked out of the window at a night sky full of stars.

And took up my pen and wrote 'Creative Carelessness'.

Because it was written so quickly, it took a long time for me to submit it to an editor, as I thought it must need to be 'worked on' before it was worthy to be considered. But it refused to be changed and within months of my making the decision to send it anyway, it had been published in the 'Worship Live' periodical, then taken into the Christian Aid anthology 'Harvest for the World' and into 'What a World', an anthology on creation published by Granary Press.

Which must prove that occasionally first inspiration is the right one.

THEY cannot take away your sky, Lord,
though they try –
with their toxic gas emissions
and their CFC pollutions
and their smog-creating smoke clouds.

It's still there.
Blue and black
in day and night-time.
Sun and moon and stars that glisten.
Clouds that glow and glower and rumble.
Sunset flare and sunrise glory
ever changing
yet eternal.
Yours, Lord.
How dare we ignore it,
as if nothing we could do will permanently harm it?

Make us aware of our responsibilities.

They cannot take away your earth, Lord,
or its worth.
With their underground nuclear testing
and their careless deforestation
and their war-torn mass destruction.
It's still there.
Rainbow coloured
plants and animals,
trees and fruit and birds and fishes,
grass and grain and sparkling water,
land and sea and soaring mountain –
your provisions
for your children.

Yours, Lord.
How dare we misuse it,
as if we need do nothing to protect it?

Make us aware of our stewardship.

Please, Lord,
before it's too late.

SUNSET *(with apologies to the late Sir John)*

When we lived on the outskirts of Bradford we were members of the Woodhouse Grove Circuit of the Methodist Church. The circuit decided to hold an event to celebrate the talents of its members and one of the Ministers – a very persuasive Welshman – suggested that it should be known as the 'Eisteddfod'. He thought that the event should be solely for the children and young people, but the committee firmly believed that adults would also want to join in the fun. The committee proved to be right.

So, every two years, there was great activity and friendly(?) rivalry as people competed in classes ranging from collage to choirs and baking to Bible reading.

There was always a class entitled grandly 'the composition of a poem' and one year the theme set for those over the age of twenty-one was 'Sunset'. At the time, I had been steeping myself in the works of the late Sir John Betjeman – with this inevitable result.

But it does make a point.

SEE the reds, the pink, the orange –
how incredibly they glow –
in the sky above the valley
where the burger bars now grow.

All the bored and busy people
hurrying to their Habitats,
never see the sunset glory
from their top floor tower block flats.

'Coronation Street' and 'Neighbours'
keep them busy after tea,
while outside the sunset's glory
blazes out with none to see.

Look above your Laura Ashley.
See the sky of gold and pink.
God with his eternal paintbox
just beyond your kitchen sink.

AS DAWN IS BREAKING IN THE SKY

'Never discard a good idea' is advice often given to writers.

Many years ago the Women's Institute organisation in my original home county of Durham set up a poetry competition for the local area. Entries were to be written about some part of the county and were restricted to members only. Both my mother and mother-in-law were members and urged me to give them some ideas. I wrote a poem myself, but it did not qualify for entry and was relegated to a file at the back of a drawer.

The poem reflected how I felt about the county of Durham, which had been heavily polluted and partly destroyed by coal mining, but was now returning to its original state as collieries were closing, waste tips were being dismantled, and the area was becoming green again. Two lines of my poem read –

> *'waste tips clad in coat of green,*
> *nature turns the pages back.'*

That image and the last line stayed with me, tucked away in the back of my mind, until I began to write a hymn on the theme of 'the dawn of a new hope' as my entry for the 'Worship Live' fifth anniversary hymn competition in 2000.

As DAWN is breaking in the sky
and darkness creeps away,
the world awakes to light and life
and thankful Christians pray,
for God renews our trust again
as night turns into day.

As scars we leave upon the land
are changed again to green,
when nature turns the pages back
with seeds that slept unseen;
then God renews the earth again
and recreates the scene.

As pain and sorrow, hurt and grief
are touched by Christian care,
which in compassion reaches out
to answer anguished prayer;
then God renews our hope again
by showing he is there.

So let us join to praise the God
who meets our daily needs
and dedicate ourselves again
to Christian words and deeds,
as we renew the vows we made
to follow where he leads.

SHELTERED DALE (8.6.8.6.8.6.) *Traditional German*

As dawn is break-ing in the sky and dark-ness creeps a-way,___ the world a-wakes_ to light and life and thank-ful Christ-ians pray,___ for God_ re-news_ our trust a-gain_ as night turns in-to day.___

SUNRISE – SUNSET

We had shared together in our church's weekend conference at Scargill House in the Yorkshire Dales and different groups had prepared sections of the closing act of worship in the chapel. Over the weekend we had been comparing the journey of our Christian faith to the stages of the day.

The choir had been rehearsing their beautiful piece for some time, before it was decided that a set of prayers was needed to fit between the verses. So, with roughly an hour to spare, I was briefed on theme, content and length and left to get on with the writing. When called in for a rehearsal, I was informed that the middle section needed to be adjusted for length and that I had failed to use the words 'stand firm' in the original version, which needed to be included as that was the song the choir would be singing behind me. That left about ten minutes to put it right before the worship began.

God has some very ingenious ways of guiding us, I know, but I'd never seen him in that particular kind of editorial role before.

At the rising of the sun, Lord, we stumble into your light.

As the dawn unravels and reveals new horizons, we step out hesitantly, unsure of our footing yet determined to move on.

So it is with our faith.

New understanding dawns, our spirits lift and enthusiasm fires. We discover new perspectives on life.

Lord, help us never to forget those first steps of faith and the promise they offered.

* * * * *

In the sunlight, nature is at its best. Colours shimmer, flowers display, birds sing and perfume fills the air. Until a cloud casts shadow and the scene darkens.

So it is with our faith.

Father, in the light of your Son we too can step out and grow, filling the air around us with light, colour and sound. We display your creative love with the creative spark you have placed in each of us.

Lord, help us to remember the sunlight, especially when the clouds begin to gather and our faith falters in the darkness.

* * * * *

At the setting of the sun, nature settles for sleep, quiet comes and shadows lengthen. Colours blaze briefly as day ends.

So it is with our faith.

Lord, there are times when we need a resting place, a quiet time when we reflect and fold into our faith as the silence and darkness enter our lives.

Lord, help us to trust in you as you guide us in darkness, comfort us in silence and meet us in the shadows. Show us how to stand firm in our faith, whatever happens.

HARVEST

Perhaps the reason why many folk come to church for the traditional harvest festival services is that it is so good to walk into a church full of the enticing smells of fruit and vegetables and to see such overwhelming displays of colour and variety. It lifts the spirits and inspires thanksgiving.

This prayer celebrates the sights and scents, but leads on to the other harvests that are all part of God's creative plan.

'We struggle to include all our gratitude in one prayer.'

Thanks be to God.

God of all light and colour, we praise you for the glories of red and yellow, green and gold and all the many shades of this harvest season.

We thank you for red apples, purple grapes and green cabbages,

for oranges and lemons, peas and barley, beans and beetroot,

for the great variety of fruit and vegetables from harvests around the world.

We may not have had a hand in growing them, but we appreciate the dedication and hard work of the people who do.

The harvest of the earth is easily recognisable and a joy to all.

Yet your harvests are far more wide-ranging than these.

God of all creation, we would also thank you for the creative powers of others:

for intelligent and logical minds working on solutions to problems;

for engineers and inventors, designers and mechanics, advisers and teachers;

for artists and musicians, writers and performers, cooks and craft workers.

The harvest of creativity is so wide, because you have given each of us the ability to be creative.

God of all love, we would thank you for the harvest of caring;

for doctors, nurses, the ambulance, police and fire and rescue services;

for workers in the power and water industries

and for all who work to serve us day by day;

for charity and welfare workers,

those who work for justice and freedom

and those who challenge us to have a conscience.

God of so many harvests, we struggle to include all our gratitude in one prayer.

Help us to live our lives in appreciation of all that your life offers to us.

SENSITIVE GOD

God's creation is full of beauty and wonder and reaches out to all our senses, but not everyone can appreciate that. Sometimes this is because the naturally beautiful things are taken for granted and we need to be taught to open our eyes and our ears to what is all around us.

For some, this teaching is essential. As I wrote this I was remembering watching a deaf/blind child being encouraged to connect with his bewildering world.

SENSITIVE God,
conductor of musical bird-song,
painter of cloud shapes and sunsets,
planter of pine-scented forests,
grower of mouth-watering melons,
unfurler of soft, silky rose petals,
awaken all our senses to the variety and extravagance of your world.

As we rejoice in the many ways we can see, hear, smell, taste and touch your
creation, make us also aware of those who lack one or more of these senses.
Lead us, caring God, to the discovery of sensitive ways in which we can help all
your children to enjoy the beauty and variety which you have provided for us.

MOTHERING GOD

In these days, when parental roles merge, it is not so easy to identify clearly the 'mothering' or 'fathering' figure in a child's life. But the images of a mother cradling and comforting her child are strong in picture and memory, even for those who have no personal experience of it.

There are some situations where the mother-love of God is essential, as cradling and comforting are the surest ways to show Christian love. Mother Teresa understood that when she reached out to touch the desperate people she worked for in the slums of Calcutta.

MOTHERING God,
there are times when we need to nestle into your arms
as a child needing comfort.
Nothing else can soothe us,
but the knowledge that you know and care about us.
Help us in our times of unease or distress
and reassure us with your love.

We pray for all those who need you in this way.
Open our eyes to all those who seek for solace
as they search for you.
Help us to help them
to find their way into your love.

AND STILL THEY COME

It is a well-known, but sad, fact that 'charity fatigue' can set in at any time. There are so many good causes making a bid for our money. We are bombarded with images of starving children and refugees. Envelopes and appeal leaflets drop through the letterbox at frequent intervals. Street collections and beggars are a daily hazard to pedestrians.

We respond to these appeals for money in different ways. Some people give a little to a lot of charities. Others make larger donations to a selected number of favourite causes. Some people don't give anything to anyone.

Where does 'charity fatigue' end and selfishness begin?

ANOTHER staring face.
Another bloated belly.
Stick insect legs and arms
and hungry, haunted eyes.
Another curled-up corpse.
Another helpless mother
flicking with weakened hands
swarming, persistent flies.

Another bloody war.
Another teenage soldier
bewildered by it all,
yet fired by thoughtless zeal.
Another shell-shot home.
Another helpless mother
powerless to influence
what heartless leaders feel.

Another rubbish tip.
Another small child scrabbling,
searching the careless scraps
that affluence throws away.
Another cardboard shack.
Another helpless mother
treasures each grain of rice,
food for a coming day.

Another charity.
Another begging letter.
An envelope, a flag,
a function to attend.
Another child in need!
Another helpless mother!
I think I've done enough –
go somewhere else, my friend!

WHO'S RIGHT?

One of the most alarming aspects of our so-called western 'civilisation', at this time, is the aggression that many people believe is necessary to secure them their 'rights'. Of course, we must fight against injustice and maladministration, but money now rules most of these issues and the aggression is constantly used to extract as much as possible from organisations and individuals by threat of prosecution.

Contrast this with those in real need, who are powerless to make any difference at all to their situation and feel that no one else cares.

One	RIGHT!
Two	Right!
Three	Rights!
Four	Rights!

One	All right!
Two	I'm right!
Three	My rights!
Four	What rights?

One	My world's fine!
Two	My world's the right one!
Three	My world belongs to me!
Four	My world is hopeless!

One	I don't have problems!
Two	I have all the answers!
Three	I don't take 'no' for an answer!
Four	I don't ask questions!

One	I've got a good lifestyle.
Two	I've got the right attitude.
Three	I get everything that's due to me.
Four	I've got nothing.

One	My life is comfortable.
Two	My life is fulfilling.
Three	My life is my own.
Four	My life's not worth living.

One	Religion means nothing to me.
Two	Religion is for good people
Three	Religion would cramp my style.
Four	Religion doesn't apply to me.

One	God? Not necessary!
Two	God? He knows I'm right!
Three	God? Only if he's on my side!
Four	God? Where are you?

One	Right!
Two	Right!
Three	Rights!
Four	Rights!

One	I am all right.
Two	I am always right.
Three	I demand my rights.
Four	I have no rights.

Questioner   Who is right? What are rights? And who will face a righteous God
without fear?

PROGRESS

*The anthology 'Wisdom is Calling' was published by Canterbury Press in 1999 to
look forward to the new millennium from a perspective of faith. But, in order to look
forward, it is sometimes necessary first to look back.*

*If our Christian dating system is set from the birth of Christ, even with a little
inaccuracy, then that birth should have made a significant difference to the world.*

Of course, it has. But have we progressed as far as we might have done?

So MANY years ago that Child was born.
The world was different then.
No science – of the kind we know.
Technology was primitive,
medicine based on herbs and folklore
and charity chiefly given at the discretion of the rich,
or in obedience to the Jewish law.
Poor people had so little to give.

Now, in our time, the world has changed.
Science has broken down barriers,
given us a space programme and weapons
and pesticides and pollutions, along with its benefits.
Technology can speak to the world in microseconds
and make life easier for those who can afford it.
Medicine brings wonder drugs with unknown side effects,
or, alternatively, still relies on herbs and folklore
and charity is occasionally given at the discretion of the rich,
or extracted from the poor with promises of riches of their own,
or two seconds of television fame in a fund-raising marathon.

How many years before we learn
the lessons that the Christ Child came to bring?
Or will our progress always be tainted
and obstructed by self-interest?

EACH GROAN OF PAIN

If the radio is switched on while I am in the kitchen I am usually only half listening to it and mainly concentrating on whatever I am doing. Occasionally the sound breaks through my concentration and I hear something that grips my attention. One morning I found myself listening to a vivid account of cruel torture, which was very hard to shut out and almost impossible to forget.

The first verse of this hymn grew directly out of that situation.

Usually I write hymns to a known tune, but this one almost set itself to a metre that reflected the sombre content of the words. The last two lines in the first four verses are a partial answer to those who claim that they cannot believe in a God who allows suffering to happen.

EACH groan of pain from tortured lips,
each tear that falls from anguished eyes,
the slightest murmur of a sigh,
as yet another victim dies,
are nails into the hands of Christ
counting against the tyrant's lies.

Each agony of starving death,
each haunted look of gaunt despair,
the scrabbling hands that search the dirt
although the earth is cracked and bare,
are echoes in the mind of Christ
of his last agonising prayer.

Each home destroyed by missile blast,
each terror of a war-torn land,
the crying of a frightened child
alone without a loving hand,
are spears pierced in the side of Christ
and pain which he can understand.

Each empty mind, which sees no pain,
each ignorance of crying need,
the pleas of those who go unheard
while others wallow in their greed,
are thorns upon the brow of Christ
and open wounds that tear and bleed.

Each healing touch relieving pain,
each voice, which speaks aloud for peace,
the giving hearts and willing hands
working so poverty may cease,
are living out the words of Christ,
striving to give his love release.

BANNERMAN (8.8.8.8.8.8.)

Paul Bateman (1954–)

Each groan of pain from tor-tured lips, each tear that

falls from an - guished eyes, the slight-est mur - mur of a

sigh, as yet a - no-ther vic - tim dies, are nails in - to the hands of

Christ count-ing a - gainst the ty - rant's lies. Each a - gon -

GRIEVING GOD

If we are driven sometimes to weep over the state of the world, how much more must God grieve?
Will we ever learn?

GRIEVING God, how often you must weep over your world,
as Jesus wept over Jerusalem.

What good we could do
and how little of it is ever done.
You help us to discover so many advantages –
technology, travel, creativity and skills –
and yet so often we use them for our own selfish ends
rather than being inspired by your overwhelming generosity.

Teach us to be more aware and alert to the needs of others,
so that your despair over our behaviour
may be turned into joy.

THE TWO-POUND COIN

Church treasurers everywhere in Britain must have rejoiced when the two-pound coin was introduced as the highest value currency coin in circulation. Now, surely, those people who had always dropped a single pound coin into the collection plate would recognise that costs had risen. So, if the two-pound coin was reflecting this in everyday terms, then this new coin must be the one to offer to God.
Some of those treasurers are now very disillusioned people.
Questions about giving money away are not easy to answer. How much? How often? Who needs it most? Will it go to the right place? What about my own needs? And the future?
Because we have certain expectations of standards of living, we often conveniently forget that we live in the richer part of the world. Many other countries and people would consider themselves wealthy if they had a third of our money and possessions.
Are we entitled to keep it to ourselves?

One   HEY! There's a coin down here. It's a two-pound coin! That'll boost the collection this week. It'll look odd among all the pound coins and fifty-pences, but I'll put it in anyway.

Two   Hey! You can't do that. It's mine!

One   How do you know that?

Two   It's mine. It belongs to me. It came out of my pocket.

One	But it doesn't have your name on it.
Two	Of course it doesn't. Don't be silly. It doesn't have anybody's name on it.
One	Yes it does. Look at it.
Two	Where?
One	There! Round the face.
Two	Oh, you mean the Queen. Yes. Well it's got her name on it of course.
One	So it means it belongs to her.
Two	No, it doesn't.
One	But it's got her name on it.
Two	I know! But that's just because it's a British coin and she's the Queen.
One	So, it's not hers?
Two	No!
One	Well it's got some other writing on it. Look! Round the edge.
Two	(*reading*) 'Standing on the shoulders of giants.'
One	Then the coin belongs to the giants!
Two	Now you're being really silly. There aren't any giants.
One	How about the giants of industry? Or commerce? The bankers? That's it! The coin belongs to the bankers.
Two	No, it doesn't! It belongs to me. The bank gave it to me.
One	Why?
Two	Because it was in my bank account. It was my money. I earned it. So it belongs to me.
One	But, look! There's some more writing on it. It's in Latin.
Two	Oh, this is ridiculous! Let's see. (*Spells it out*) D_E_I G_R_A oh, I can't be bothered with that. What does it mean?
One	Well, I know D_E_I spells Dei – that means God. That's it! The coin belongs to God!
Two	No, it doesn't! The coin belongs to me. What on earth would God want with my money, anyway?
One	Precisely! What on earth would God want to do with our money?

GENEROUS GOD

God understands our insecurity and our attitude to money, but he asks us to trust him and to continue to share with others.

Generous God, you ask us to trust in you for everything.
But it's so hard to do that.
We've learned to trust the money in our pockets
to put a roof over our heads,
food on the table
and to provide all the luxuries we feel we can afford –
and some we can't.
It's difficult to know how we would manage otherwise.

Father, forgive us our lack of trust.
If we had no money we would have to depend on you.
Help us to remember this
and, with that knowledge,
to understand that you are depending on us
to be open-handed with what we have,
on your behalf,
towards those who are trusting
that you will provide for them.

CREATOR GOD

Prejudice is a cruel word. Whether it be prejudice against someone of a different colour, or social background, or intellectual ability; or the stronger prejudice against people of a different faith, or sexual orientation, or belonging to a hated nation; all prejudice creates hostility and misunderstanding. Or even worse things.

God created a diverse world and we may struggle to understand why some people are the way they are, or behave in the way that they do.

We live in God's world and only he can help us to begin to understand its complexities.

Creator God,
the world you gave us is so diverse
that its complexities may never be unravelled,
so extravagant that its riches may never be spent,
and so extraordinary that we find it a constant source of amazement.

Yet, when we come to people, we expect it all to be so simple.
As if everyone made in your image should look and act the same.

God of many faces,
help us to rejoice in our diversity,
to be prepared to be understanding about other people's complexities,
to be generous in our dealings with others
and to be amazed at the new revelations you give to us each day.

We cannot all agree about everything –
that would be unrealistic –
but we can follow the pattern set by Jesus,
who accepted all who were prepared to take up his cross
and be obedient to your will.

Understanding and all-knowing God,
as we travel the road of faith together,
keep our minds open and our hearts united,
so that barriers fall and images fade
as we join in the worship and work of your kingdom.

WORLD WIDE WEB

The stunning photographs of planet earth taken from outer space, plus memories of the school classroom globe marked by the lines of latitude and longitude, are the two images that fed this poetic prayer.
We have the capability to destroy it.
Will we?

Our map-drawn world is a spinning blue-green ball
caught in a linear cage of grid references.

If a single line is broken
will the ball spin
out of control
into oblivion?

Or will lines
ruptured by violence
open the hole
which finally spills life
out from our planet
into mass destruction?

Lord, help us to remember our connectedness!

GOD OF DAWN

As the third millennium dawned and pictures from across the world were beamed into our television sets, there was a general air of celebration and a universal hope that people of this new era would have learned lessons from the past.

Now, four and a half years later, that sense of optimism has been smothered by events calculated to wreak havoc. Terrorism, war, famine, crime, disease and countless other catastrophes have dimmed the light and depressed the high spirits.

God brings a new dawn to each day. The sun rises to defeat the shadows and God's world is filled with the glory of light once again.

The world may be full of troubles, but God calls us to renew our faith again each day and to move on into the future with him.

GOD of dawn, each day's renewal
brings the world into your light.
As your sun defeats the shadows,
drives away the darkest night:
we would greet this new beginning
as your call to start again,
lead us on with hope and courage,
make your will and purpose plain.

Christ, you walked the world as we do,
knew its human pain and loss.
As your love broke through the barriers
by your death upon the cross;
we still speak your gospel message,
though two thousand years have gone.
Help us now translate its meaning
in this present world of wrong.

Holy Spirit, inspiration,
light and truth and root of prayer,
as your challenge moves us forward
taking us we know not where:
we will follow your direction,
though the way may not be clear.
Shape us, change us, recreate us,
so the future holds no fear.

Praise to God, who spoke creation,
giving life to time and space.
Praise to Christ, whose living presence
showed the world your human face.
Praise the Spirit, daily witness
to your ever-loving way.
Take us now and reawake us,
challenge us to use this day.

IN CONVERTENDO (8.7.8.7.D.) *Peter Cutts (1937–)*

God of dawn, each day's re - new - al brings the world in -to your light. As your sun de - feats the sha - dows, drives a - way the dark - est night: we would greet this new be - gin - ning as your call to start a - gain, lead us on with hope and cou - rage, make your will and pur - pose plain.

ONE WORLD

On that fateful day, September 11th 2001, none of us could really believe what we were seeing or hearing as the twin towers collapsed in New York. The loss of life was appalling, although thankfully many people did manage to escape. But the event was so vividly and cruelly dramatic that it will never be forgotten. It also created a great sense of fear in cities throughout the world, as civilised nations realised that no one was safe from such terrorist acts.

Yet devastating as that event was, it was not the only act of terrorism to take place that year, or since then. All over the world people are being killed indiscriminately. Natural disasters create havoc in many places. Dictators make life hellish under their rule. Evil is everywhere.

Bewildered by it all, we can only turn to God for guidance.

CREATOR God, whose world is one family, help us to recognise our common humanity.

For wherever they are, victims of terrorism cry out in bitter anguish; bombs and shells kill soldiers and civilians alike; homes and businesses are shattered and broken; rescuers search rubble for faint signs of life; bereaved children weep bewildered tears; family units are torn apart by destruction; refugees lose their dignity and sense of identity; peace is shattered.

Keep us alert to the tears and fears that are our common experience. Open our hands and hearts in sympathy and understanding. Show us how to express our care in practical ways. Please, Lord.

God of peace, whose world is torn apart by evil, greed, power and cruelty, help us to be active in our work for peace.

For all over your world power corrupts and greed distorts values; evil has no conscience; terrorists justify actions by perverted logic; prejudice feeds fear and fear promotes violence; weapons of mass destruction are dangerously active; ignorance promotes hostility, danger is at hand.

Help us to find the truth behind the propaganda. Teach us to promote peaceful ways and positive thoughts. Give us the courage to tackle prejudice where we find it. Show us how to face up to evil and defeat it. In your name, Lord and for your sake.

PEACE IS ...

An anthology entitled 'Timeless Prayers for Peace' would be expected to have its main focus as peace between nations and peoples.

But there are many ways in which we use the word 'peace'.

PEACE is the resolution of conflict
as we make our peace.

Peace is the struggle for harmony
as we live in peace.

Peace is being set free from anxiety
as we are left in peace.

Peace is our Christian calling
as we share the Peace.

Peace is our blessing from worship
as we go in peace.

Peace is God's final resolution
as we rest in peace.

POPPIES

Our friend the Welsh Minister has been mentioned already, earlier in this section of the book. His manse was not far from our home and we were walking past his garden one day and admiring his beautiful display of yellow flowers.

'They're Welsh poppies,' he said. 'I'll give you a few to take home with you.'

Experienced gardeners will know what happened next. It was just like the kind of parable Jesus might have told to the crowds.

From a Welsh friend came native poppies –
yellow flowers and a few shoots –
brought to keep memories green and give them roots.

A bare patch in the garden they filled –
or would when fully grown.
Once planted, they were left alone.

Next year, they grew and flourished
bringing yellow sunshine to that space
and smiling memories of a friendly face.

In two years yellow flowers appeared garden-wide.
Wind-blown and bird-scattered,
Welsh wizardry grinned at us from every side.

Soon neighbours' gardens, boundary walls
and cracked paving stones had their share.
Green shoots and budding heads and yellow flowers –
our friend is everywhere.

Unchecked, those seeds by friendship sown will spread.
Look at the flowers and learn – as Jesus said.

TIME

Time is measured and regulated and passes at the same speed each minute, hour and day.

Our perception of time is a different matter altogether. If we are waiting for something to happen, time can appear to pass very slowly. If we are particularly busy, or enjoying a special occasion, time seems to fly. Young people are eager to grow up: older people find it difficult to believe how many years have passed. Historians look back and point at significant lessons that we should learn: scientists predict a future that sometimes does not seem to offer a great deal of hope.

'Help us Lord, to put our time into your perspective.'

Time runs in circles and cycles.
Day follows night; weeks turn into months, then months into years.
One generation follows another.
Our lives are locked and linked by time.

God of all time, we thank you that you have been the eternal truth throughout
   history.
We are grateful for the generations that have gone before us, especially for those
   people of vision, imagination and creativity.
We recognise the legacy of those who have made great discoveries;
      those who have invented and improved equipment and machinery;
      those who expanded medical knowledge
      and for all who have fought to eradicate injustice, poverty and disease.
We recognise your hand in their lives and especially in the hearts and minds of
      those who have passed on their faith in an unbroken line leading to our day.

Yet today we know that there are still discoveries to be made and problems to be
      solved.
Our world is far from perfect. In fact, it often seems as if things are getting worse.

Help us, Lord, to put our time into your perspective.
When we despair, let us recognise the signs of hope.
When we feel we cannot cope, help us to remember that we have come through
      difficult times before and that you are always there to help us.
When we believe that nothing will ever change, teach us that cycles and circles
      turn and return and that you are constantly in the centre radiating your love,
      compassion and guidance.

And the future, Lord?
We leave that in your hands, but recognise that our hands will play a part in
      shaping it.
Help us not to betray your trust in us, but to be prepared to take our place in your
      circle of time.

GOD THE WEAVER

This is the hymn from which the title of this book was taken. It has the last place in this collection because, in only four verses, it sums up so much of the previous writing. It reflects the story of my life, but many others will find their own reflections there too. The story of its writing and the steps to its publication provide important stepping stones along my personal way through the multi-coloured maze.

I wrote this piece for two friends, a Minister and his wife, who were being called out from our Methodist Circuit at short notice, in order to fill an unexpected vacancy for a Superintendent Minister in another circuit. This was a disturbing event causing disruption to the family and heartache to our friends, who did not really want to leave.

So the lines of the third verse were particularly written for them as reassurance that, wherever they were, they would be supported by a loving network of Christian friends. Rosemary and Peter were moved by this, one of many farewell gifts they received. After they had left the hymn was used occasionally, but largely forgotten.

Some time afterwards I was asked to lead a drama workshop for a church weekend in another circuit of the city – the same weekend mentioned earlier in the book as the source of my hymn 'Come sing a song of faith'. It was arranged that the leader of the music workshop, David McCarthy, would give me a lift to the preparatory meetings and the weekend itself. David was a Local Preacher colleague in our circuit, but he also happened to be an exceptional musician and a composer who had already written many hymn tunes.

At this time I was at the stage of beginning to wonder whether I really had a gift for writing and if I should explore this further. All my life I had scribbled away at all kinds of material. I had been a Methodist Local Preacher since the age of twenty. Local radio had given me the opportunity to contribute material to their 'God slot' and I had begun to write one or two hymns and some short drama pieces for worship. Was God trying to tell me something? And, if so, what was the next move?

With great hesitation I decided to take the opportunity to ask David McCarthy to look at this hymn 'God the weaver'. It had already been received quite enthusiastically by those who had used it, but I needed the opinion of someone who had a wide experience of good hymn writing. As David had already set some of Fred Pratt Green's words to music, I believed that David should be the one that I should approach. But it was a very nerve-racking thing to do. At least, if he needed to tell me that my work was hopeless, then that could be done face to face and I should be able to see his reaction.

The script was carefully prepared, sealed in an envelope and tucked away in the folder I was carrying. On the way to the first meeting I decided to leave it there until the return journey. As we approached the end of my road on the way back, I decided that it was now or never. The car pulled up outside our house and I thrust the envelope at David, garbling something like, 'I've written this. It's probably rubbish. Would you look at it, please?' and ran up the steps to the safety of my own front door. He must have thought he was dealing with a mad woman.

But, maybe not.

I heard nothing from him until it was time for the next meeting, so I had no idea what to say as I got into the car. He gave me an envelope, which I hardly dared to open. Inside was my hymn – and the tune he had written for it. David McCarthy is not the kind of man who would have wasted time writing that music if he had not thought the piece was worth it.

When we arrived at the church he searched out a piano, so that I could hear how the tune sounded. On the way home we discussed the next steps I should take. Although my first approach to Stainer & Bell was encouraging, it was fruitless, as they had no plans for publishing single items, nor were there any new hymn books being produced at that time. However, I had been given that extra confidence that helped me to see and seize opportunities to use my writing skills. Contributing prayers to the West Yorkshire Synod books was one step. Writing material for special weekends and events was another. Then, a few years later, Stainer & Bell began to publish the periodical 'Worship Live' and the first hymn of mine that they published was 'God the weaver'. From that time the writing world opened up to me in many new ways.

How wonderful it is to serve a God who will not always give us a straight answer, but will weave the pattern and pull together the strands that make up the tapestry of our lives. There have been many people in the pattern of my life who have helped me to take steps along the way – some of them have been mentioned in the book, but there are many, many others and I am profoundly grateful to them, and to God for giving me the opportunity to make them a part of the picture. Together we make up a truly multi-coloured maze.

GOD the weaver, making patterns,
spinning threads throughout our days –
joy and sadness interwoven,
strands of sorrow, strands of praise.
Help us to discern your weaving
in the multi-coloured maze.

Teach us, Lord, to trust your guidance
when the pattern is not clear,
and to feel your strength and comfort
when life's fabric's torn by fear.
Help us sense that in the dark times
lightening love is always near.

When we see the pattern changing
and a new direction starts,
let us know your love unbroken
winds through life in all its parts
by the threads of love and friendship
closely woven in our hearts.

Though we never see the picture
with your sense of space and time,
help us, Lord, to take our places
in our faith's continuing line,
as all lives are interwoven
in your final grand design.

PERSPECTIVE (8.7.8.7.8.7.) *David McCarthy (1931–)*

God the wea - ver, mak - ing pat - terns, spin - ning
threads through-out our days – joy and sad - ness in - ter -
-wo - ven, strands of sor - row, strands of praise. Help us
to dis - cern your weav - ing in the mul - ti - co - loured maze.

Index of Hymns with Tunes

Index of Themes

*Separate items beginning on the same page are identified
by roman numerals after the page number.*

Christian life

Age   44, 48, 53, 58, 91, 94, 96(i), 98, 106, 140, 141(i), 141(ii), 142(i), 142(ii), 143, 144, 145(ii)

Being changed   32, 37, 39, 40, 53, 59, 76, 78, 98, 102, 110, 113, 122(iii), 123, 127(i), 127(ii), 132(i), 134, 135, 138(ii), 152, 160, 162, 167, 170(i), 174, 176(i), 178, 179

Blame   22, 63, 78, 128, 129, 154, 168

Call   37, 40, 44, 48, 58, 66, 90(i), 90(ii), 91, 96(ii), 100, 114, 160, 174

Commitment   2, 5, 44, 58, 76, 88, 91, 96(ii), 103, 106, 108(i), 108(ii), 125, 145(i), 145(ii), 154, 160, 174

Enthusiasm   37, 38, 39, 40, 44, 53, 94, 103, 116, 138(i), 142(ii), 155, 177

Everyday life   102, 120(ii), 121(i), 122(i), 122(ii), 124(i), 126(i), 126(ii), 132(ii), 141(i), 141(ii), 142(i), 145(ii), 152, 179

Forgiveness   34, 63, 78, 82, 128, 130, 132(i)

Guilt   22, 78, 82, 113, 128, 130, 134, 165, 166, 167, 170(i), 170(ii)

Healing   72, 113, 127(ii), 128, 129, 130, 132(i), 133, 136, 139, 145(ii), 160, 168

Hope   34, 72, 78, 82, 84, 91, 127(i), 132(i), 148, 152, 155, 158, 160, 174, 178, 179

Inspiration   37, 39, 40, 94, 96(i), 100, 138(i), 164(i)

Money 15, 56, 64, 65, 66, 70, 108(i), 108(ii), 109, 157, 165, 166, 167, 170(ii), 172(i)

Stepping out in faith   44, 48, 54, 58, 59, 74, 83, 90(i), 90(ii), 91, 106, 116, 123, 132(i), 162, 172(i), 172(ii)

Troubles   72, 84, 113, 127(ii), 128, 129, 130, 133, 134, 136, 140, 141(i), 141(ii), 143, 144, 145(i), 145(ii), 148, 149, 150, 152, 162, 164(ii), 166, 168, 176(i), 179

Trust   44, 50, 74, 84, 91, 114, 127(i), 127(ii), 162, 172(i), 178, 179

Work   28, 32, 58, 116, 122(iii), 126(ii), 163, 178

Youth   44, 53, 58, 66, 70, 91, 94, 96(i), 98, 106, 120(i), 121(i), 121(ii), 122(ii), 124(ii), 142(ii)

Church life

Advent/Christmas   2, 4, 5, 8, 10, 12, 14, 125

Anniversary   106, 178

Baptism   2, 120(i)

Breaking bread   102

Death and funerals   145(i), 145(ii), 148, 149, 150, 152, 176(i)

Family of God   90(ii), 91, 96(i), 98, 99, 102, 110, 112, 113, 114, 120(i), 120(ii), 121(i), 122(i), 122(ii), 124(ii), 125, 129, 130, 132(i), 132(iii), 136, 139, 140, 142(ii), 143, 145(i), 145(ii), 149, 152, 157, 162, 164(ii), 166, 167, 168, 170(i), 172(ii)

Flower festival   111, 177

Harvest Festival   163

House of prayer   15, 103, 110

Lent/Easter   15, 22, 28, 32, 33, 34, 36, 78

Lord's Prayer   63

Pentecost   37, 38, 39, 40, 78, 81

Wedding   124

Worship and preaching   88, 96(ii), 100, 103, 114, 116, 160, 163, 174

God

Creator   88, 100, 154, 155, 157, 158, 159, 160, 162, 163, 164(i), 172(ii), 174

With many faces   53, 83, 90(i), 90(ii), 91, 94, 96(i), 98, 99, 109, 116, 122(iii), 123, 133, 136, 138(i), 139, 145(i), 152, 157, 164(i), 164(ii), 170(i), 172(i), 172(ii), 176(i), 178, 179

Holy Spirit

Breath of God   39, 154, 174

Pentecost   37, 38, 39, 40

Jesus Christ

Birth   2, 4, 5, 8, 10, 12, 14

Carpenter   28, 32

Easter   34, 36, 72, 78, 136

Good Friday   28, 32, 33, 34, 72, 108, 136, 148, 168

Holy Week   15, 22, 34, 36

Ministry   56, 58, 65, 70, 123, 136, 174, 177

Bibliography

A World of Blessing
An anthology of benedictions and prayers from every continent and many cultures, compiled by Geoffrey Duncan
ISBN 1 85311 332 8
Canterbury Press, 2000

Courage to Love
An anthology of inclusive worship material on human sexuality, edited by Geoffrey Duncan
ISBN 0 232 52405 X
Darton, Longman and Todd, 2002

Faith for the Future
An anthology of hymns and tunes compiled for the 150th anniversary of the Methodist Local Preachers Mutual Aid Association, published in 1999 and available from the LPMAA, 89 High Street, Rickmansworth, Hertfordshire WD3 1EF

First Fruits
An Anglican Stewardship Association anthology on the subjects of generosity and giving
ISBN 1 85311 392 1
Canterbury Press, 2001

Harvest for the World
An anthology edited by Geoffrey Duncan for Christian Aid
ISBN 1 85311 461 8
Canterbury Press, 2002

Let Justice Roll Down
An anthology for Lent edited by Geoffrey Duncan for Christian Aid and CAFOD
ISBN 1 85311 555 X
Canterbury Press, 2003

Life with God and **Open with God**
Two collections, containing prayers for all occasions and situations, published by West Yorkshire Synod (WYS) books, available from District Office, West Yorkshire District, 19 Wentworth Court, Rastrick, Brighouse, West Yorkshire HD6 3XD

NewStart Hymns and Songs
A collection of hymns primarily written for the Millennium
ISBN 1 84003 327 4 (Full music)   ISBN 1 84003 326 6 (Words edition)
Kevin Mayhew, 1999

Seeing Christ in Others (1st edition)
Edited by Geoffrey Duncan
ISBN 1 85311 192 9
Canterbury Press, 1998

Seeing Christ in Others (2nd edition)
An extended edition of the above
ISBN 1 85311 441 3
Canterbury Press, 2002

Songs for the New Millennium
ISBN 0 7151 4930 X (Full music)   ISBN 0 7151 4931 8 (Words edition)
Methodist Publishing House, 1999

Sound Bytes
94 songs for the 21st century for children to share with everyone – a great book for anyone working with children from about seven upwards
ISBN 0 85249 856 X (Full music)   ISBN 0 85249 857 8 (Words edition)
Stainer & Bell, 1999

Timeless Prayers for Peace
Edited by Geoffrey Duncan
ISBN 1 85311 515 0
Canterbury Press, 2003

What a World
An illustrated anthology on ecology and the environment, compiled and edited by Geoffrey Duncan, with textile art by Pamela Pavitt, and published by the imprint of the United Reformed Church
ISBN 0 85346 212 7
Granary Press, 2002

Wisdom is Calling
Edited by Geoffrey Duncan
ISBN 1 85311 243 7
Canterbury Press, 1999

Worship Live
A journal of new worship material of all kinds, published by Stainer & Bell three times a year and available by subscription

Acknowledgements

Page 88 | The tune LITTLE CORNARD (Martin Shaw) is reprinted by kind permission of J. Curwen & Sons Limited, 8/9 Frith Street, London W1D 3JB.

Page 95 | Scriptures and additional materials quoted are from the *Good News Bible* © 1994 published by the Bible Societies/HarperCollins Publishers Ltd, *UK Good News Bible* © American Bible Society 1966, 1971, 1976, 1992. Used with permission.

Pages 96 and 106 | The hymn texts *Lord, you call us to your service* and *God of past generations* are reprinted by kind permission of the Methodist Local Preachers Mutual Aid Association, 89 High Street, Rickmansworth, Hertfordshire WD3 1EF.

Page 114 | The hymn text *Christian people, sing together* is reprinted by kind permission of Kevin Mayhew Ltd, Buxhall, Stowmarket, Suffolk IP14 3BW.

Page 150 | The hymn text *Here in this place we meet with you in sorrow* is reprinted by kind permission of CJM Music Ltd, Don Bosco House, Coventry Road, Coleshill, West Midlands B46 3EA.